English for Listening, Speaking, Reading & Writing

JN433378

NEW CONNECTION

BRING YOUR ENGLISH TO THE NEXT LEVEL

TEACHER'S GUIDE 2

INTRODUCTION

Welcome to ***NEW CONNECTION*** — *BRING YOUR ENGLISH TO THE NEXT LEVEL.* This is the second book in a series created to propel learners toward fluency. Outstanding English skills will open up doors for anyone in today's world. No matter how out of reach a student's learning goals seem to be, the ***NEW CONNECTION*** series will provide the boost he or she needs.

Each unit of ***NEW CONNECTION*** — *BRING YOUR ENGLISH TO THE NEXT LEVEL* follows a set structure designed to push students to put what they have learned into practice as well as to challenge them to expand their skills. The unit begins with a **Words & Expressions** section, which utilizes both audio and visual methods to introduce words and expressions related to the topic. This is followed by a **Listen Up** exercise. At this time, learners will review vocabulary by answering questions based on a dialogue or monologue. The **Act It Out** section then gives learners a chance to put the vocabulary to use with a partner.

Students will move on to a video clip in which actors use new vocabulary — in addition to new grammar points and expressions — in real-life situations. They will listen along and fill in blanks too, and later be tested for comprehension. Afterwards, they're prompted to put freshly learned vocabulary and grammar skills to use in a series of review exercises. The unit ends with a related article and an opportunity for students to write their own compositions.

As students progress through each level, they are constantly encouraged to put what they have learned to use. At the same time, they never stop taking on new challenges to help themselves reach the next benchmark in the learning process. By developing a hunger for advancement, ***NEW CONNECTION*** — *BRING YOUR ENGLISH TO THE NEXT LEVEL* proves that the sky is the limit for today's learners.

CONTENTS

CONTENT CHART

Unit	Title	Subject	Conversation	Grammar
1	**Meeting People**	School Clubs	Good to Meet You / Meet the Coach	Simple Present Tense
2	**Time to Eat**	Food	Enjoy Free Food	Count Nouns vs. Non-Count Nouns
3	**Living with Technology**	Electronics	Homework or Video Games?	Present Continuous Tense
4	**Looking Good**	Physical Appearance	A Trip Home	Simple Past Tense
5	**Not Feeling So Good**	Symptoms	Feeling Sick?	Linking Verbs Causative Verbs
6	**The Big Screen**	Types of Movies	Movie Night	Talking about Time
7	**How Do You Feel?**	Feelings	Bad News, Good News	Participial Adjectives
8	**All in Good Fun**	Hobbies	Making Plans	Gerunds and Infinitives
9	**Game Time**	Sports	Sports Talk	Past Continuous Tense
10	**Rain or Shine**	Weather	A Weekend at the Lake	Simple Future Tense
11	**Eating Out**	Food	Dinner Date	Indefinite Pronouns
12	**School Life**	Characteristics	Tell Me What to Do	Conditionals

	Reading	Writing
Statements Third Person Singular Yes / No Questions Wh- Questions	A Strange College Club	Personal Profiles
Differences Plural Count Nouns Articles, Determiners & Quantifiers	Eat More and Lose Weight	Festivals
Statements Questions Verb + -ing Usage	It's a YouTube World	Internet Language
Be Verbs Verbs	Dangerous Beauty	Wanted Ads
Definition Usage	Natural Medicine for Your Cold	Medical History
Prepositions Questions Telling Time	The Wildest Job in Movies	Movie Reviews
Usage Paired Adjectives Past Participial Adjectives with Prepositions	Do Animals Have Feelings?	Life Stories
Usage Signal Words Different Meanings	Make Your Life More Extreme	Pastimes
Statements Questions Usage	Sports Hero	Favorite Sports
Statements Questions Be Going to vs. Will Future Time Expressions	Safe at Home	Storm Warnings
	Going to Restaurants around the World	Restaurant Reviews
Zero Conditional First Conditional Different Forms	Working for No Money	Job Applications

LEARNING OVERVIEW

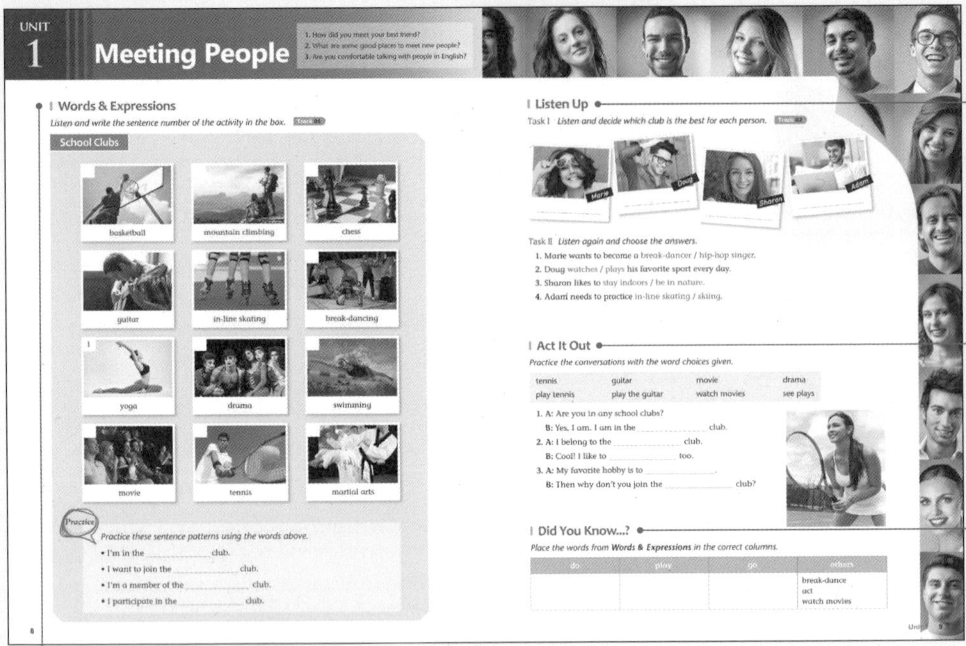
UNIT 1 Meeting People

1. How did you meet your best friend?
2. What are some good places to meet new people?
3. Are you comfortable talking with people in English?

Words & Expressions

Listen and write the sentence number of the activity in the box.

School Clubs

basketball · mountain climbing · chess · guitar · in-line skating · break-dancing · yoga · drama · swimming · movie · tennis · martial arts

Practice

Practice these sentence patterns using the words above.

- I'm in the ______ club.
- I want to join the ______ club.
- I'm a member of the ______ club.
- I participate in the ______ club.

Listen Up

Task I *Listen and decide which club is the best for each person.*

Marie · Doug · Sharon · Adam

Task II *Listen again and choose the answers.*

1. Marie wants to become a break-dancer / hip-hop singer.
2. Doug watches / plays his favorite sport every day.
3. Sharon likes to stay indoors / be in nature.
4. Adam needs to practice in-line skating / skiing.

Act It Out

Practice the conversations with the word choices given.

tennis	guitar	movie	drama
play tennis	play the guitar	watch movies	see plays

1. A: Are you in any school clubs?
   B: Yes, I am. I am in the ______ club.
2. A: I belong to the ______ club.
   B: Cool! I like to ______ too.
3. A: My favorite hobby is to ______.
   B: Then why don't you join the ______ club?

Did You Know...?

Place the words from **Words & Expressions** *in the correct columns.*

do	play	go	others
			break-dance act watch movies

Listen Up
checks students' understanding of the words they have learned through listening comprehension questions.

Act It Out
helps students understand the key expressions and words by practicing short dialogues.

Did You Know...?
helps students expand their vocabulary through words and expressions.

Words & Expressions
provides useful items with audio support to further students' understanding of the topic.

Conversation
includes a video clip helping students understand the content.

Review
checks students' understanding of the passage.

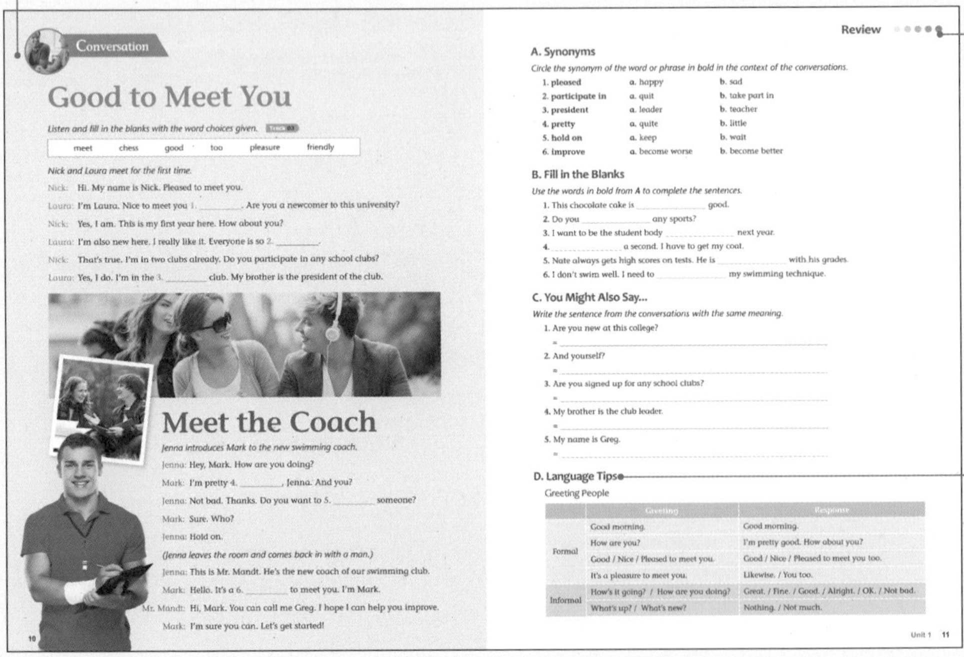
Conversation

Good to Meet You

Listen and fill in the blanks with the word choices given.

meet	chess	good	too	pleasure	friendly

Nick and Laura meet for the first time.

Nick: Hi. My name is Nick. Pleased to meet you.
Laura: I'm Laura. Nice to meet you 1. ______. Are you a newcomer to this university?
Nick: Yes, I am. This is my first year here. How about you?
Laura: I'm also new here. I really like it. Everyone is so 2. ______.
Nick: That's true. I'm in two clubs already. Do you participate in any school clubs?
Laura: Yes, I do. I'm in the 3. ______ club. My brother is the president of the club.

Meet the Coach

Jenna introduces Mark to the new swimming coach.

Jenna: Hey, Mark. How are you doing?
Mark: I'm pretty 4. ______, Jenna. And you?
Jenna: Not bad. Thanks. Do you want to 5. ______ someone?
Mark: Sure. Who?
Jenna: Hold on.
(Jenna leaves the room and comes back in with a man.)
Jenna: This is Mr. Mandt. He's the new coach of our swimming club.
Mark: Hello. It's a 6. ______ to meet you. I'm Mark.
Mr. Mandt: Hi, Mark. You can call me Greg. I hope I can help you improve.
Mark: I'm sure you can. Let's get started!

Review

A. Synonyms

Circle the synonym of the word or phrase in bold in the context of the conversations.

1. **pleased** a. happy b. sad
2. **participate in** a. quit b. take part in
3. **president** a. leader b. teacher
4. **pretty** a. quite b. little
5. **hold on** a. keep b. wait
6. **improve** a. become worse b. become better

B. Fill in the Blanks

Use the words in bold from A to complete the sentences.

1. This chocolate cake is ______ good.
2. Do you ______ any sports?
3. I want to be the student body ______ next year.
4. ______ a second. I have to get my coat.
5. Nate always gets high scores on tests. He is ______ with his grades.
6. I don't swim well. I need to ______ my swimming technique.

C. You Might Also Say...

Write the sentence from the conversations with the same meaning.

1. Are you new at this college?
2. And yourself?
3. Are you signed up for any school clubs?
4. My brother is the club leader.
5. My name is Greg.

D. Language Tips

Greeting People

	Greeting	Response
Formal	Good morning.	Good morning.
	How are you?	I'm pretty good. How about you?
	Good / Nice / Pleased to meet you.	Good / Nice / Pleased to meet you too.
	It's a pleasure to meet you.	Likewise. / You too.
Informal	How's it going? / How are you doing?	Great. / Fine. / Good. / Alright. / OK. / Not bad.
	What's up? / What's new?	Nothing. / Not much.

Language Tips
provides everyday English usage and sentence structure.

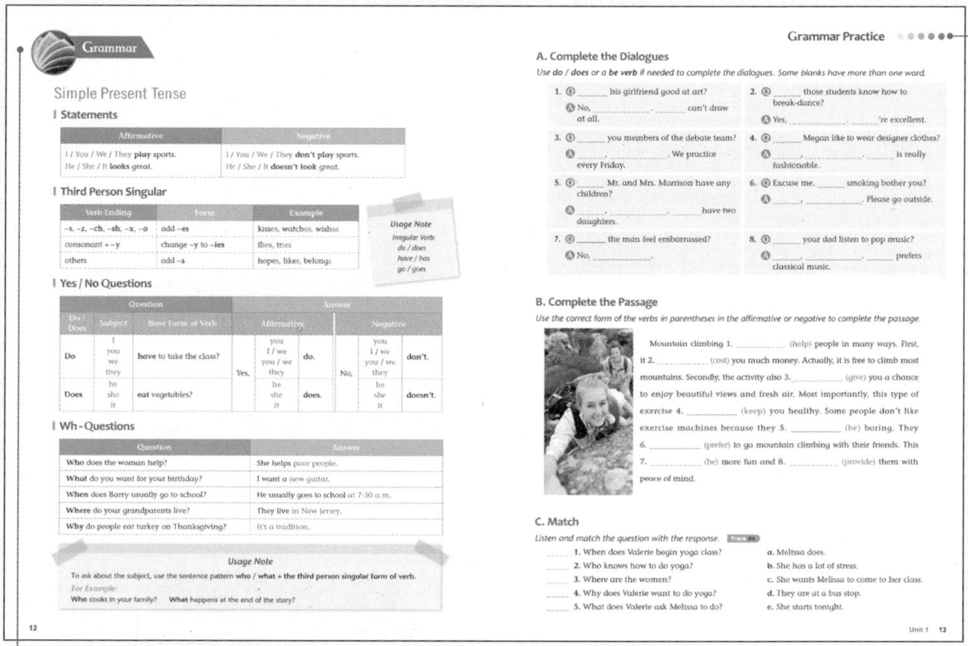

Grammar Practice

enables students to practice grammar in context to enhance accuracy and fluency.

Grammar

presents essential grammar to build overall accuracy.

Reading

enables students to broaden their knowledge through interesting articles.

After You Read

confirms students' understanding of the passage.

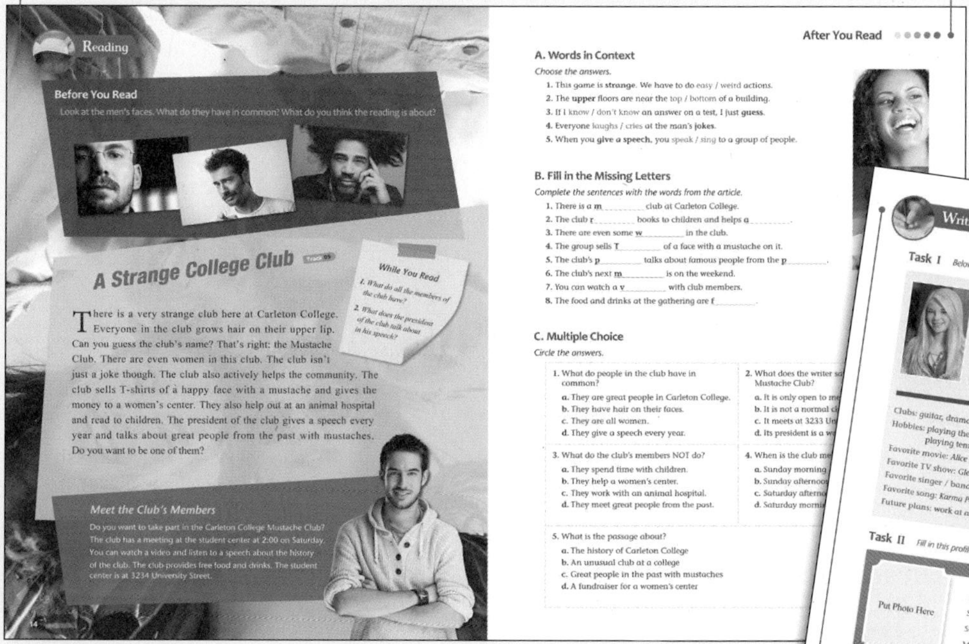

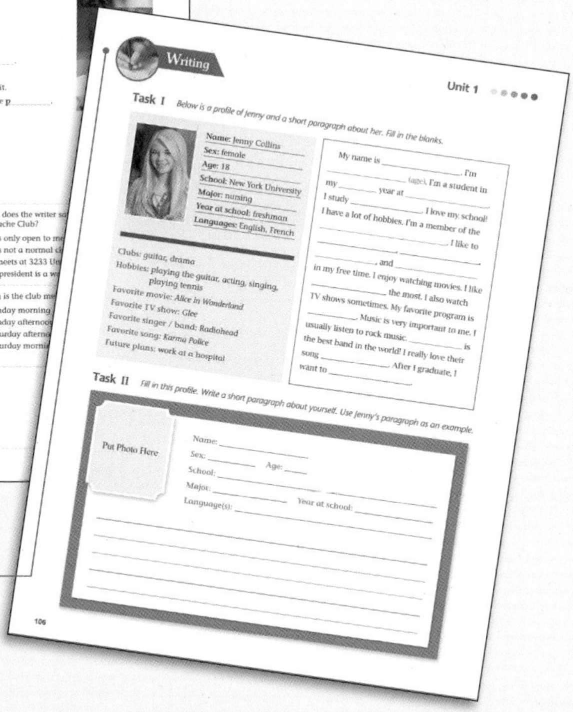

Writing

provides an opportunity for students to practice acquired language in authentic discourse using personalized content.

Meeting People

Words & Expressions

Listen and write the sentence number of the activity in the box. Track 01

School Clubs

11

basketball

7

mountain climbing

2

chess

6

guitar

9

in-line skating

10

break-dancing

1

yoga

5

drama

3

swimming

8

movie

12

tennis

4

martial arts

Practice

Practice these sentence patterns using the words above.

- I'm in the **chess** club.
- I want to join the **guitar** club.
- I'm a member of the **drama** club.
- I participate in the **tennis** club.

Teaching Resources

Audio Transcripts for *Words & Expressions*: Track 01

1. I feel relaxed when I do **yoga**.
2. I enjoy **chess** because it makes me think.
3. **Swimming** makes your whole body strong.
4. Many people learn **martial arts** to protect themselves.
5. Hillary wants to be an actress, so she studies **drama**.
6. Playing **guitar** always makes me feel happy.
7. I enjoy **mountain climbing** because I like fresh air.
8. Comedies are my favorite type of **movie**. I like to laugh.
9. Let's go **in-line skating** in the park.
10. **Break-dancing** is popular among teenagers.
11. Many tall people play **basketball**.
12. Alex likes watching **tennis** on TV.

More to Teach:

Who Does It?

Sport / Activity	Person
basketball	basketball player
mountain climbing	mountain climber
chess	chess player
guitar	guitar player / guitarist
in-line skating	in-line skater
break-dancing	break-dancer
yoga	yoga practitioner
drama	actor / actress
swimming	swimmer
movie	moviegoer
tennis	tennis player
martial arts	martial artist

For Example:

Jared **plays guitar** in a band, but he's not a very good **guitarist**.

My sister loves **playing tennis**. She's a great **tennis player**.

1. How did you meet your best friend?
2. What are some good places to meet new people?
3. Are you comfortable talking with people in English?

Listen Up

Task I *Listen and decide which club is the best for each person.* Track 02

break-dancing

basketball

mountain climbing

in-line skating

Task II *Listen again and choose the answers.*

1. Marie wants to become a break-dancer / hip-hop singer.
2. Doug watches / plays his favorite sport every day.
3. Sharon likes to stay indoors / be in nature.
4. Adam needs to practice in-line skating / skiing.

Act It Out

Practice the conversations with the word choices given.

tennis	guitar	movie	drama
play tennis	play the guitar	watch movies	see plays

1. A: Are you in any school clubs?
   B: Yes, I am. I am in the tennis/guitar/movie/drama club.
2. A: I belong to the tennis/guitar/movie/drama club.
   B: Cool! I like to play tennis/play the guitar/watch movies/see plays too.
3. A: My favorite hobby is to play tennis/play the guitar/watch movies/see plays .
   B: Then why don't you join the tennis/guitar/movie/drama club?

Did You Know...?

*Place the words from **Words & Expressions** in the correct columns.*

do	play	go	others
yoga martial arts	basketball chess guitar tennis	mountain climbing in-line skating swimming	break-dance act watch movies

Teaching Resources

Audio Transcripts for *Listen Up*: Track 02

Speaker 1: **Marie**

I listen to hip-hop music. I like Jay-Z the most. I want to become a **break-dancer**.

Speaker 2: **Doug**

Basketball is my favorite sport. I **play** it every day. I hope I can play basketball in college.

Speaker 3: **Sharon**

I **enjoy nature** and I love to go **mountain climbing**. The view from Jade Mountain is beautiful.

Speaker 4: **Adam**

My friends are good at **in-line skating**. I want to join them, but I need to practice first.

More to Teach:

When to Use Articles

The way we talk about playing sports is different from how we talk about playing musical instruments. When talking about sports, we never place the article **the** between **play** and the **sport name**. For instruments, we can say it either way.

For Example:

Henry **plays** basketball. Jenny **plays** (the) violin.

Word Usage: Do vs. Play vs. Go

Verb	Usage	Example
do	for sports that don't require equipment	Christine **does aerobics** every day. On Tuesdays, I usually see groups of people **doing tae kwon do** in the park.
play	for team sports or games where there is a winner and loser	I love to **play badminton**. Neil **plays volleyball** with his friends at lunch. Laura doesn't like to **play golf**. It's too difficult for her.
go	for sports that end in **–ing**	Every winter, my family and I **go skiing** in the Rockies. My brother and I like to **go diving** in the Philippines. Let's **go running** in the hills tomorrow morning.

Usage Note

The sports that end in **–ing** can also be used in their verb form:

to jog	to swim	to snowboard	to dive	to fish
to run	to ski	to in-line skate	to climb	to hike

For Example:

I **go jogging** in the morning before I go to work. (I **jog** in the morning before I go to work.)

Conversation

Good to Meet You

Listen and fill in the blanks with the word choices given. Track 03

meet	chess	good	too	pleasure	friendly

Nick and Laura meet for the first time.

Nick: Hi. My name is Nick. Pleased to meet you.

Laura: I'm Laura. Nice to meet you 1. **too**. Are you a newcomer to this university?

Nick: Yes, I am. This is my first year here. How about you?

Laura: I'm also new here. I really like it. Everyone is so 2. **friendly**.

Nick: That's true. I'm in two clubs already. Do you participate in any school clubs?

Laura: Yes, I do. I'm in the 3. **chess** club. My brother is the president of the club.

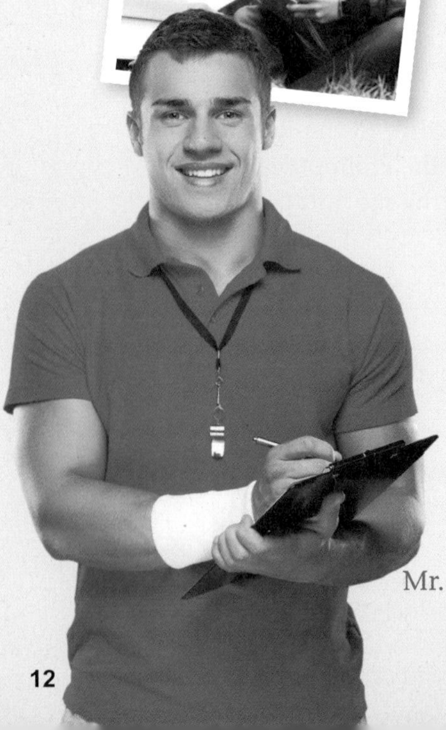

Meet the Coach

Jenna introduces Mark to the new swimming coach.

Jenna: Hey, Mark. How are you doing?

Mark: I'm pretty 4. **good**, Jenna. And you?

Jenna: Not bad. Thanks. Do you want to 5. **meet** someone?

Mark: Sure. Who?

Jenna: Hold on.

(Jenna leaves the room and comes back in with a man.)

Jenna: This is Mr. Mandt. He's the new coach of our swimming club.

Mark: Hello. It's a 6. **pleasure** to meet you. I'm Mark.

Mr. Mandt: Hi, Mark. You can call me Greg. I hope I can help you improve.

Mark: I'm sure you can. Let's get started!

Key Words

❶ **meet** *v.*

I can't wait to meet all of my new classmates.

EXTENSION **Other Usage of *Meet*:**

Glenda meets her English tutor at four o'clock on Thursdays. (means *see somebody at a set time and place*)

❷ **pleased** *adj.* | synonyms | happy, glad |

Kevin is pleased with his new phone. It has many functions.

EXTENSION **please** *v.*

Don't try to please everyone. Just be yourself.

pleasure *n.*

Nick gets a lot of pleasure from learning new languages.

❸ **newcomer** *n.*

Do you know the newcomer's name?

❹ **friendly** *adj.* | synonyms | nice, kind |

Everyone in this country is very friendly.

❺ **participate in** *phr.* | synonym | take part in |

Dean is quite active. He participates in lots of school activities.

❻ **president** *n.*

Margo is the president of the drama club.

EXTENSION **Other Usage of *President*:**

The nation's president often speaks on TV. (means *a head of a country or a company*)

❼ **coach** *n., v.*

I don't like our basketball coach. He yells at us all the time.

Mike coaches a high school baseball team.

❽ **introduce** *v.*

Your friends are all beautiful. Can you introduce me to them?

EXTENSION **Other Usage of *Introduce*:**

The teacher introduces the lesson topic at the start of the class. (means *give basic ideas*)

❾ **hold on** *phr.*

Hold on! Let me go inside and get your phone for you.

❿ **improve** *v.*

Seth's French improves every day because he studies really hard.

A. Synonyms

Circle the synonym of the word or phrase in bold in the context of the conversations.

1. **pleased** (a.) happy b. sad
2. **participate in** a. quit (b.) take part in
3. **president** (a.) leader b. teacher
4. **pretty** (a.) quite b. little
5. **hold on** a. keep (b.) wait
6. **improve** a. become worse (b.) become better

B. Fill in the Blanks

*Use the words in bold from **A** to complete the sentences.*

1. This chocolate cake is **pretty** good.
2. Do you **participate in** any sports?
3. I want to be the student body **president** next year.
4. **Hold on** a second. I have to get my coat.
5. Nate always gets high scores on tests. He is **pleased** with his grades.
6. I don't swim well. I need to **improve** my swimming technique.

C. You Might Also Say...

Write the sentence from the conversations with the same meaning.

1. Are you new at this college?
   = **Are you a newcomer to this university?**
2. And yourself?
   = **How about you? / And you?**
3. Are you signed up for any school clubs?
   = **Do you participate in any school clubs?**
4. My brother is the club leader.
   = **My brother is the president of the club.**
5. My name is Greg.
   = **You can call me Greg.**

D. Language Tips

Greeting People

	Greeting	Response
Formal	Good morning.	Good morning.
	How are you?	I'm pretty good. How about you?
	Good / Nice / Pleased to meet you.	Good / Nice / Pleased to meet you too.
	It's a pleasure to meet you.	Likewise. / You too.
Informal	How's it going? / How are you doing?	Great. / Fine. / Good. / Alright. / OK. / Not bad.
	What's up? / What's new?	Nothing. / Not much.

Simple Present Tense

Statements

Affirmative	Negative
I / You / We / They **play** sports. He / She / It **looks** great.	I / You / We / They **don't play** sports. He / She / It **doesn't look** great.

Third Person Singular

Verb Ending	Form	Example
–s, –z, –**ch**, –**sh**, –x, –o	add –**es**	kisses, watches, wishes
consonant + –**y**	change –**y** to –**ies**	flies, tries
others	add –**s**	hopes, likes, belongs

Usage Note
Irregular Verb:
do / does
have / has
go / goes

Yes / No Questions

Question			Answer					
Do / Does	Subject	Base Form of Verb	Affirmative			Negative		
Do	I you we they	**have** to take the class?	Yes,	you I / we you / we they	**do.**	No,	you I / we you / we they	**don't.**
Does	he she it	**eat** vegetables?	Yes,	he she it	**does.**	No,	he she it	**doesn't.**

Wh-Questions

Question	Answer
Who does the woman help?	She helps poor people.
What do you want for your birthday?	I want a new guitar.
When does Barry usually go to school?	He usually goes to school at 7:30 a.m.
Where do your grandparents live?	They live in New Jersey.
Why do people eat turkey on Thanksgiving?	It's a tradition.

Usage Note

To ask about the subject, use the sentence pattern **who** / **what** + **the third person singular form of verb.**

For Example:

Who cooks in your family? **What** happens at the end of the story?

A. Complete the Dialogues

*Use **do** / **does** or a **be verb** if needed to complete the dialogues. Some blanks have more than one word.*

1. Q **Is** his girlfriend good at art?
   A No, **she isn't**. **She** can't draw at all.

2. Q **Do** those students know how to break-dance?
   A Yes, **they do**. **They** 're excellent.

3. Q **Are** you members of the debate team?
   A **Yes**, **we are**. We practice every Friday.

4. Q **Does** Megan like to wear designer clothes?
   A **Yes**, **she does**. **She** is really fashionable.

5. Q **Do** Mr. and Mrs. Morrison have any children?
   A **Yes**, **they do**. **They** have two daughters.

6. Q Excuse me. **Does** smoking bother you?
   A **Yes**, **it does**. Please go outside.

7. Q **Does** the man feel embarrassed?
   A No, **he doesn't**.

8. Q **Does** your dad listen to pop music?
   A **No**, **he doesn't**. **He** prefers classical music.

B. Complete the Passage

Use the correct form of the verbs in parentheses in the affirmative or negative to complete the passage.

Mountain climbing 1. **helps** (help) people in many ways. First, it 2. **doesn't cost** (cost) you much money. Actually, it is free to climb most mountains. Secondly, the activity also 3. **gives** (give) you a chance to enjoy beautiful views and fresh air. Most importantly, this type of exercise 4. **keeps** (keep) you healthy. Some people don't like exercise machines because they 5. **are** (be) boring. They 6. **prefer** (prefer) to go mountain climbing with their friends. This 7. **is** (be) more fun and 8. **provides** (provide) them with peace of mind.

C. Match

Listen and match the question with the response. Track 04

e	1. When does Valerie begin yoga class?	a. Melissa does.
a	2. Who knows how to do yoga?	b. She has a lot of stress.
d	3. Where are the women?	c. She wants Melissa to come to her class.
b	4. Why does Valerie want to do yoga?	d. They are at a bus stop.
c	5. What does Valerie ask Melissa to do?	e. She starts tonight.

Teaching Resources

Audio Transcripts for *Grammar Practice*:

C. Match Track 04

Melissa: Hey, Valerie. What's up?

Valerie: Not much, Melissa. I have a yoga class tonight.

Melissa: You do yoga? No way!

Valerie: Well, it's my first day. I can't wait.

Melissa: That's great. I also do yoga. It's fun, and it gives me more energy.

Valerie: Cool.

Melissa: It also makes my muscles stronger.

Valerie: I want to try yoga because I have a lot of stress. Does yoga help with that?

Melissa: Yes. It keeps you calm and helps you focus too.

Valerie: Do you still do yoga?

Melissa: No, but I want to start another class.

Valerie: Come to my class.

Melissa: That sounds good. Maybe I can go with you someday.

Valerie: Good. This is my bus, so I have to go. Give me a call!

ANSWER KEY Student's Book ▶ p. 14

Reading

Before You Read

Look at the men's faces. What do they have in common? What do you think the reading is about?

A Strange College Club

Track 05

While You Read

1. What do all the members of the club have?

2. What does the president of the club talk about in his speech?

There is a very strange club here at Carleton College. Everyone in the club grows hair on their upper lip. Can you guess the club's name? That's right: the Mustache Club. There are even women in this club. The club isn't just a joke though. The club also actively helps the community. The club sells T-shirts of a happy face with a mustache and gives the money to a women's center. They also help out at an animal hospital and read to children. The president of the club gives a speech every year and talks about great people from the past with mustaches. Do you want to be one of them?

Meet the Club's Members

Do you want to take part in the Carleton College Mustache Club? The club has a meeting at the student center at 2:00 on Saturday. You can watch a video and listen to a speech about the history of the club. The club provides free food and drinks. The student center is at 3234 University Street.

Key Words

❶ strange *adj.* antonyms: usual, normal, ordinary

The way the man speaks is a little strange.

❷ club *n.*

She belongs to a book club. They meet every Saturday morning.

EXTENSION **Other Usages of *Club*:**

We can go to a club after dinner on Friday. (means *a place where people go to dance*)

The golf club is half price now. You should buy it. (means *a long stick used in golf*)

❸ grow *v.*

Brad's girlfriend doesn't want him to grow his hair long.

EXTENSION **Other Usages of *Grow*:**

People's hair turns gray as they grow old. (means *become*)

Many farmers in this town grow rice. (means *make plants develop*)

❹ upper *adj.*

A famous actor lives on the upper floor of the building.

❺ mustache *n.*

The old man has a big brown mustache.

EXTENSION **Usage Note:**

A **mustache** is hair on one's upper lip, while a **beard** refers to the hair on one's cheeks and chin. People with beards usually have mustaches too.

❻ joke *n., v.*

Sharon tells funny jokes. She always makes her friends laugh.

It's rude to joke about someone's weight.

EXTENSION **play a joke (on someone)**

Sam likes to play jokes on his classmates. He often hides their things.

❼ give / make / deliver a speech *phr.*

The leader is a good public speaker. He delivers powerful speeches.

EXTENSION **Usage Note:**

When describing the topic of a speech, we often use the words **on** or **about**. Jane often gives speeches **on** the use of English idioms.

❽ free *adj.*

The hotel offers a free bus service to and from the airport.

EXTENSION **Other Usages of *Free*:**

Everyone is free to give their opinions. (*adj.* not controlled)

Are you free to talk now? I have a few questions to ask you. (*adj.* not busy)

The report is free of errors. It's perfect. (*phr.* not have)

A. Words in Context

Choose the answers.

1. This game is **strange**. We have to do easy / weird actions.
2. The **upper** floors are near the top / bottom of a building.
3. If I know / don't know an answer on a test, I just **guess**.
4. Everyone laughs / cries at the man's **jokes**.
5. When you **give a speech**, you speak / sing to a group of people.

B. Fill in the Missing Letters

Complete the sentences with the words from the article.

1. There is a **mustache** club at Carleton College.
2. The club **reads** books to children and helps **animals**.
3. There are even some **women** in the club.
4. The group sells **T-shirts** of a face with a mustache on it.
5. The club's **president** talks about famous people from the **past**.
6. The club's next **meeting** is on the weekend.
7. You can watch a **video** with club members.
8. The food and drinks at the gathering are **free**.

C. Multiple Choice

Circle the answers.

1. What do people in the club have in common?
   a. They are great people in Carleton College.
   (b.) They have hair on their faces.
   c. They are all women.
   d. They give a speech every year.

2. What does the writer say about the Mustache Club?
   a. It is only open to men.
   (b.) It is not a normal club.
   c. It meets at 3233 University Street.
   d. Its president is a woman.

3. What do the club's members NOT do?
   a. They spend time with children.
   b. They help a women's center.
   c. They work with an animal hospital.
   (d.) They meet great people from the past.

4. When is the club meeting?
   a. Sunday morning
   b. Sunday afternoon
   (c.) Saturday afternoon
   d. Saturday morning

5. What is the passage about?
   a. The history of Carleton College
   (b.) An unusual club at a college
   c. Great people in the past with mustaches
   d. A fundraiser for a women's center

NOTES

UNIT 2

Time to Eat

ANSWER KEY Student's Book ▶ p. 16

Words & Expressions

Task I *Listen and write the words in the blanks.* Track 06

beef	rice	cereal	pork	mangoes	broccoli	carrots
cheese	yogurt	pears	onions	chicken	corn oil	potatoes

rice

chicken

corn oil

pears

broccoli

cheese

Task II *Write the words from **Task I** to match the pictures.*

beef

potatoes

mangoes

onions

yogurt

carrots

cereal

pork

Practice

Talk to a partner.

- Do you eat foods from the six groups every day?
- What foods from the list do you like to eat?
- Which fruits do you eat? How about vegetables?
- Do you eat meat? What is your favorite kind of meat?

Teaching Resources

Audio Transcripts for *Words & Expressions*: Track 06

1. I have a cold. I want to eat some **chicken** soup.
2. Shelly bakes delicious pies, especially from **pears**.
3. I don't use a lot of **corn oil** in my cooking; it's not healthy!
4. **Rice** is the most popular grain in Asia.
5. **Broccoli** and other vegetables are good for you.
6. Goat **cheese** is white, and it's usually salty.

More to Teach:

Animals and Meats

Some meats have a different name from the animal. Here are the most common meats:

Name of Animal	Meat
cow	beef
sheep	mutton
pig	pork
hen	chicken

Nouns that Can Be *Count* and *Non-Count*

Food (Non-Count)	Animal (Count)
chicken, lamb, fish	a chicken, a lamb, a fish
I want to have some **chicken** for dinner.	They have some **chickens** on their farm.

Non-Count	Count (Means A Kind / Piece of)
food, fruit, salad, wine, hair	a food, a fruit, a salad, a wine, a hair
Sean loves to eat **fruit**. She has very long **hair**.	I only eat two **fruits** — apples and strawberries. (two kinds of fruit) There is a **hair** on your shirt. (one piece of hair)

Usage Note

E-mail can be *count* or *non-count*. It is also used to mean "e-mail account."
I get a lot of **e-mail** every day. (I get a lot of **e-mails** every day.)
I check my **e-mail** every day. (I check my **e-mail account** every day.)

1. What's your favorite food?
2. Do you have a healthy diet?
3. Can you draw a food pyramid?

Listen Up

Task I *Listen and choose the correct shopping list.* Track 07

☐ **List A**
pineapples
beef
yogurt
potatoes
carrots
kiwis
broccoli
oranges
rice

☑ **List B**
beef
yogurt
potatoes
onions
kiwis
broccoli
oranges
pears
apples

☐ **List C**
yogurt
chicken
potatoes
kiwis
broccoli
pears
rice
onions
noodles

Task II *Listen again and fill in the blanks with the words you hear.*

1. Vince plans to **cook** dinner for his **girlfriend**.
2. Vince's girlfriend likes to eat **meat**, especially **beef**.
3. The main dish is beef with **broccoli**. There is also a yogurt and **onion** sauce.
4. Laura wants to cook some **rice**, but Vince decides to cook **potatoes**.
5. Vince uses **fruit** to make salad for **dessert**.

Act It Out

Practice the conversations with the word choices given.

meat / vegetables / seafood

pork / beef / lamb / green beans / broccoli / fish / shrimp

breakfast / lunch / dinner

egg sandwiches / potato salad / beef noodle soup / rice with pork

1. **A:** Do you eat meat/vegetables/seafood?
   B: Yes, I do. I especially like pork/beef/lamb/green beans/broccoli/fish/shrimp.
2. **A:** What do you eat for breakfast/lunch/dinner?
   B: I usually eat egg sandwiches/potato salad/beef noodle soup/rice with pork.
3. **A:** Do you cook at home?
   B: Yes. I like to cook / make egg sandwiches/potato salad/beef noodle soup/rice with pork.

Did You Know...?

We can add **–y** *to certain nouns to make adjectives to describe food.*

Noun	Adjective	Noun	Adjective
taste	tasty	salt	salty
oil	oily	health	healthy
juice	juicy	cream	creamy

Fill in the blanks with the appropriate words.

1. This sauce is too **creamy**. It can make you fat.
2. I don't often eat fried food. It's very **oily**.
3. This orange is sweet and **juicy**.
4. The popcorn is **salty**. Have some water with it.

Teaching Resources

Audio Transcripts for *Listen Up*: Track 07

Vince: Laura, are you a good cook?

Laura: I'm not bad. Do you need some help, Vince?

Vince: Yeah. I want to **cook** dinner for my **girlfriend**. Any suggestions?

Laura: Does she eat **meat**?

Vince: Yes, she does. She really likes **beef**.

Laura: We can prepare beef with **broccoli** and a **yogurt** and **onion** sauce.

Vince: That sounds delicious.

Laura: We should cook some **rice** too.

Vince: She eats rice all the time. Let's cook **potatoes**.

Laura: Potatoes go well with beef. How about some **dessert**?

Vince: We can make **fruit** salad. I need **apples**, **pears**, **kiwis**, and **oranges**.

Laura: That sounds good. Can I come to your dinner too?

Vince: Maybe another time.

More to Teach:

Food Adjectives

Taste	Content	Texture	Preparation
salty	low-fat	hard	boiled
tasty	sugar-free	soft	fried
sweet	natural	oily	baked
juicy	healthy	dry	
sour			
spicy			

For Example:

This lemon ice cream is quite **sour**.

There are a lot of **sugar-free** sodas in the stores today.

The bread is good, but it's a little **dry**. Do you have any butter?

Boiled eggs are good for your health; they have less fat.

Conversation

Enjoy Free Food

Listen and fill in the blanks with the word choices given. Track 08

much	beef	left	beer	believe	steak

Jill and Rick are talking at a party.

Jill: What's up, Rick? What do you think about these burgers?

Rick: They're pretty good. Most of the food at this party is excellent. Have a 1. **steak**. They're great!

Jill: You like 2. **beef** a lot. You have two burgers and a steak on your plate.

Rick: I'm a huge beef eater.

Jill: I don't eat 3. **much** beef. I prefer fruit. I'm crazy about mangoes. I eat two or three mangoes every day.

Rick: Mangoes are OK.

Jill: Fruit is good for you, but beef is not very healthy.

Rick: Beer is not healthy either. Should I put down my bottle?

Jill: No, not at all. Have a few more bottles of 4. **beer**. It's free.

Rick: The mangoes are free too. Eat up.

Jill: Good idea. There are some more mangoes in the kitchen, right?

Rick: I 5. **believe** so. But can we go in the kitchen?

Jill: I guess so. Let's hurry. There isn't a lot of food 6. **left**. Meet me at the bar in 15 minutes.

Key Words

❶ **burger** *n.*

I like burgers with lettuce and tomatoes.

EXTENSION **Usage Note:**

A **burger** is usually a **hamburger**. It's made from beef. We can use **burger** for other sandwiches too, like **fish burger** or **chicken burger**.

---

❷ **excellent** *adj.* | synonyms | great, good, terrific, wonderful |

This wine is excellent. I really enjoy it.

---

❸ **huge** *adj.*

Frank is a huge movie fan. He loves Japanese movies.

EXTENSION **Usage Note:**

From weakest to strongest: **big → large → huge**

---

❹ **prefer** *v.*

I rarely drink coffee. I prefer tea to coffee.

Penny prefers running to swimming. She doesn't like to be in water.

---

❺ **crazy** *adj.*

My brother is crazy about cars. He really loves them.

EXTENSION **Other Usages of *Crazy*:**

She never cleans the kitchen. It drives me crazy. (*phr.* make someone angry)

I don't sleep well. I often have crazy dreams. (*adj.* strange)

---

❻ **healthy** *adj.*

Water is a very healthy drink. You should drink at least eight glasses a day.

EXTENSION **health** *n.*

You should quit smoking. It can badly damage your health.

---

❼ **either** *adv.*

I can't come to the party and Benny can't either.

EXTENSION **Adverbs to Agree:**

Used in positive sentences	**also**	after *be verbs*
		before *verbs*
		after *modal verbs*
	too	at the end
Used in negative sentences	**either**	at the end

The beautiful woman over there is a singer. She's also an actress.

Sam likes soccer and Robin does too.

Key Words

❽ not . . . at all *phr.*

A: Are you hungry?

B: No, not at all. (I'm not hungry at all.)

EXTENSION **Usage Note:**

We also use the phrase **not at all** to mean "you're welcome" or "don't mention it."

A: Thank you so much.
B: Not at all.

❾ believe *v.*

A: Is the painting worth a lot of money?

B: I believe so.

EXTENSION **belief** *n.*
Emma has a strong belief in God. She goes to church every Sunday.

❿ hurry *v.* synonym rush

We need to hurry. The show starts at five.

EXTENSION **Phrases that Use *Hurry*:**

hurry up	Hurry up! It's raining.
in a hurry synonym in a rush	He's in a hurry to get home.
There's no hurry.	There's no hurry. We have lots of time.

A. Word Definitions

Replace the words in italics with the choices given. Change the word form if necessary.

excellent	huge	prefer	healthy	hurry

1. Fruit and vegetables are *good for your body*.
   ▶ **Fruit and vegetables are healthy.**
2. The writer's new book is a *big* success.
   ▶ **The writer's new book is a huge success.**
3. I need to *go faster*. I'm late for school.
   ▶ **I need to hurry. I'm late for school.**
4. She *likes* black coffee *better*. She doesn't like to add milk or sugar.
   ▶ **She prefers black coffee. She doesn't like to add milk or sugar.**
5. This pizza is *delicious*. You're a good cook.
   ▶ **This pizza is excellent. You're a good cook.**

B. Meanings in Context

Choose the meaning of the sentence in the conversation.

1. I'm a huge beef eater. (**a.**) I eat a lot of beef. **b.** I'm big, and I eat beef too.	**2.** I'm crazy about mangoes. (**a.**) I love to eat mangoes. **b.** I feel strange when I eat mangoes.
3. Mangoes are OK. **a.** I don't like mangoes. (**b.**) They taste fine.	**4.** No, not at all. (**a.**) Absolutely not. **b.** Of course.
5. It's free. **a.** There's nothing to do. (**b.**) There's no cost.	**6.** Eat up. (**a.**) Eat more. **b.** Go upstairs to eat.

C. Language Tips

Asking about a Meal

Greeting
What do you think about / of the . . .? How do you like the . . .? How is / are the . . .? Is / Are the . . . OK?

Response		
It's / They're	excellent / great. delicious / tasty. pretty good. alright / OK. not very good. terrible.	☺ ↓ ☹

Practice the sentence patterns using the choices given.

onion rings	cheeseburgers	strawberry yogurt	baked potatoes	fried rice
spaghetti	chicken soup	chocolate cake	fruit juice	pizza

Count Nouns vs. Non-Count Nouns

Differences

	Count Nouns			Non-Count Nouns			
Definition	has a singular and plural form			only has a singular form			
Example	a potato two students	an onion four pears	one bottle five mangoes	salt time	news meat	music milk	cheese water

Plural Count Nouns

	Noun Ending	Plural Form	Example	
Regular Plurals	–s, –sh, –ch, –x, –z	add –es	buses	watches
	consonant + –y	change –y to –ies	babies	parties
	–o	add –es or –s	tomatoes	photos
	others	add –s	houses	drivers
Irregular Plurals	wife → wives child → children	man → men foot → feet	person → people mouse → mice	

Articles, Determiners & Quantifiers

Count Nouns	Non-Count Nouns
Do you want a sandwich? They have one daughter.	X
The mangoes are free.	The meat is fresh.
This / That coat is warm.	This / That soup is cold.
These / Those people are my friends.	X
I need to buy some apples.	I need to buy some medicine.
Are there any questions?	Is there any water in the bottle?
We don't have enough chairs for everyone.	I don't have enough money for a new car.
There are a lot of / lots of people at the party.	There is a lot of / lots of food left.
I don't eat many vegetables. (a large amount)	I don't eat much beef. (a large amount)
There are a few books in my bag. (a small amount)	I only want a little milk in my coffee. (a small amount)
Few people use film cameras. (a very small amount)	We have little information on this topic. (a very small amount)

A. Complete the Passage

*Use the correct articles (**a**, **an**, or **the**) to complete the passage. Put an **X** if no word is needed.*

The garden salad is 1. **a** popular dish in this restaurant. People enjoy 2. **the** dish because it's delicious. 3. **The** garden salad is really big. Each plate has 4. **X** lettuce, 5. **an** egg, and 6. **a** tomato. 7. **The** dressing is good. You can choose 8. **a/the** French kind or 9. **the/X** Thousand Island. Don't forget to ask for 10. **the** restaurant's famous blue cheese. It's nice on top of 11. **the** salad.

B. Fill in the Blanks

*Use **a few**, **a little**, **many**, **much** and the correct form of the words given to complete the sentences.*

mistake	soap	church	friend	time	money	child

1. Let's hurry. There isn't **much time** left. The train leaves in five minutes.
2. There are **many churches** in Rome. It's impossible to visit them all in one day.
3. I only have **a little money**. I can't pay for lunch.
4. Jessica is not very sociable. She only has **a few friends** at school.
5. This is terrible! I can see **many mistakes** on your math test.
6. Don't put too **much soap** in the water.
7. The Jones have **many children**. They have a total of seven.

C. Correct the Mistakes

Fix the errors in the dialogue.

Harry: Do you want to go to [^a] basketball game?

Marvin: That sounds great, but I need to go shopping.

Harry: Shopping? Really? But you are ~~the~~ **a** huge basketball fan.

Marvin: You're right, but my girlfriend's birthday is tomorrow. I want to cook ~~the~~ **a** dinner for her.

Harry: You're ~~an~~ **a** nice boyfriend. What does she like?

Marvin: I don't know. Do you have ~~many~~ **any** suggestions?

Harry: Cook some seafood ~~pastas.~~ **pasta**. It's ~~a~~ **an** easy dish to make.

Marvin: That's [^a] good idea. I can put in ~~a~~ shrimp, just ~~a few~~ **a little** white sauce, and ~~any~~ **some** noodles.

Harry: Mmm. She's ~~the~~ **a** lucky girl.

Teaching Resources

More to Teach:

Plural Nouns

	Rule	Example
1	Proper nouns ending in –y → –ys	The **Murphys** are a nice couple. (Harrys, Macys)
2	Singular and plural are the same	I have four **fish**. (sheep, deer)
3	Look like plurals but are singular	**Physics** is interesting. (mathematics, news)
4	Always plural	My **clothes** are old. (shorts, glasses)

There Is / Are

	Rule	Example
1	With *count* nouns, we use **there is** for one, and **there are** for more. With *non-count* nouns, we use **there is**.	**There is** a man at the door. (count — one) **There are** four people in the car. (count — more than one) **There is** music in the room. (non-count)
2	There is / are no + Noun = There is / are not any + Noun (more common)	**There aren't any** people in the market. (**There are no** people in the market.) **There isn't any** furniture in that house. (**There is no** furniture in that house.)

Measure Words for *Non-Count Nouns*

Non-Count	Count
A: How much **beer** is there? **B:** There's a lot of beer.	**A:** How many **bottles of beer** are there? **B:** There are three bottles of beer.
A: How much **cheese** do we have? **B:** We don't have much.	**A:** How many **slices of cheese** do we have? **B:** We have four slices.

Before You Read

Look at the pictures. Which foods do you often eat? Do you think you have a healthy diet?

Eat More and Lose Weight

Track 09

While You Read

1. What does The French Diet tell readers?

2. What foods are good for you? What foods should you avoid?

Are you sick of dieting to lose weight? Good news! Michel Montignac is a food writer and author of *The French Diet*. He says the type of food is more important than the amount of food. He divides all food into two groups, good and bad. It sounds easy, right? You don't even need to exercise too much! The good foods, like vegetables, cereals, and pasta, release sugar into the blood more slowly. They also stop the body from keeping fat. Potatoes, candy, and white flour are examples of bad foods. Try to avoid these foods. Not everyone agrees, but it is a very interesting idea, especially for food lovers who want to stay slim.

Tips for Healthy Dieting

1. Don't eat too much. Eat until you're 80 percent full.
2. Treat vegetables as the main meal and meat as a side dish.
3. Eat lots of fresh food.
4. Enjoy your meal slowly and use it as a social time.

Key Words

❶ **lose** *v.*

I don't want to lose my hair.

EXTENSION **Other Usage of *Lose*:**
Those players are terrible. They lose every game. (means *not win*)

❷ **weight** *n.*

That child is the same weight as an adult. She's too heavy.

EXTENSION **weigh** *v.*
Weigh the flour before you mix it with the water.

❸ **be sick of** *phr.* synonym | be tired of

I'm sick of taking the train to work. It's always crowded with people.

EXTENSION **sick** *adj.* synonym | ill
She can't come to class today. She is sick with the flu.

❹ **diet** *v.*

You don't need to diet. You just need more exercise.

EXTENSION **Other Usages of *Diet*:**
The diet of monkeys includes fruit, eggs, flowers, and insects. (means *a type of food*)
Sheila is on a diet. She only eats fruit now. (be on a diet = diet)
This is diet soda. It doesn't have much sugar. (means *low-fat or low-sugar*)

❺ **divide** *v.*

I divide my time between work and study.

❻ **release** *v.*

The sun releases a lot of energy.

EXTENSION **Other Usages of *Release*:**
The bears need to be released into the wild. (*v.* let go)
The singer's latest release is a success. It is selling very well. (*n.* a CD, video, film, etc.)

❼ **full** *adj.*

I'm full. I can't eat any more food.

EXTENSION **Other Usages of *Full*:**
The restaurant is full. We have to go to another one. (means *no space*)
I plan to spend two full weeks in London. (means *complete*)

❽ **social** *adj.*

He's a very social guy. He likes to meet new people.

A. Multiple Choice

Circle the answers.

1. Who is Michel Montignac?
   a. A doctor at a hospital
   (b.) A food writer
   c. A food lover
   d. A famous French cook

2. Which of these is good food?
   a. Potatoes
   b. White flour
   (c.) Cereals
   d. Candy

3. Why does Michel Montignac say that vegetables are healthy?
   a. They have a lot of sugar.
   (b.) They don't let the body store fat.
   c. They are a main meal.
   d. They don't release sugar into the blood.

4. Which is NOT a tip for healthy dieting?
   a. Stop eating before you're full.
   b. Make your meals a pleasant time.
   c. Eat lots of vegetables. Don't eat too much meat.
   (d.) Do not exercise much.

B. Words with Different Meanings

Match the word in bold with its definition.

1 Jenny and Leo are **sick** of seeing each other. They are not friends anymore. __b__
Joe is really **sick**. We should visit him in the hospital. __a__
Definition: a *adj.* not healthy b *adj.* bored, tired

2 You don't need to **diet**. You're already very slim. __b__
I want a **diet** Coke with my burger. __a__
Definition: a *adj.* having low fat or sugar content b *v.* to eat less to lose weight

3 I **exercise** at the gym three times a week. __a__
Swimming can help you **exercise** your arm and leg muscles. __b__
Definition: a *v.* to do sports activities b *v.* to train a body part

4 If you're already **full**, you can take these cookies home. __b__
This train is **full**. We have to wait for the next one. __a__
Definition: a *adj.* having no space b *adj.* having eaten enough food

C. Choose the Right Tip

Read and write the correct number from tips for healthy dieting.

1. Vegetables are a big part of Greek people's everyday diet. __2__
2. Portuguese people like to eat their meals with friends and family. __4__
3. In Indonesia, people don't like to eat canned foods. __3__
4. Japanese meals are usually smaller in size than Western meals. __1__
5. Some restaurants in Italy grow their own vegetables to offer fresh food. __3__

UNIT
3 Living with Technology

ANSWER KEY Student's Book ▶ p. 24

Words & Expressions

Listen and write the sentence number of the item in the box. Track 10

Electronics and the Internet

3 
a camera

6 
a touch screen phone

12 
an e-mail

10 
a text message

2 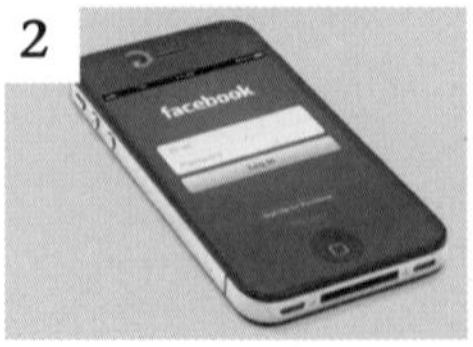

Facebook

5 

MSN messenger

7 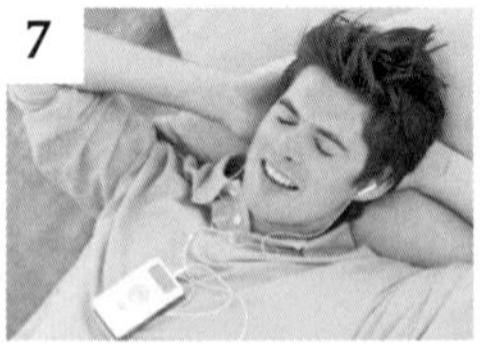
an MP3 player

9 

YouTube

1 
a printer

4 
a copy machine

8 
a laptop computer

11 
the Internet

Match the verbs / verbal phrases with the nouns above. There may be more than one match.

listen to music on	type on	send	use
take pictures with	post on	chat on	surf

Practice

Practice these sentence patterns using the words above.

- Do you know how to **take pictures with a camera** ?
- It's fun to **send a text message** .
- You can **chat on MSN messenger** and talk to your friends.
- I **listen to music on an mp3 player** every day.
- The **copy machine** doesn't work. I can't **use it** .

Teaching Resources

Audio Transcripts for *Words & Expressions*: Track 10

1. Michael can print beautiful posters with his new **printer**.
2. Gina posts something on **Facebook** every ten minutes.
3. I like to take pictures of my friends with my **camera**.
4. I need to make a few copies. Do you know how to use the **copy machine**?
5. Do you have some free time to chat online with me?
6. You can use your **touch screen phone** to play games.
7. I have a lot of new songs on my **MP3 player**.
8. James usually types up his homework on his **laptop computer**.
9. I like to watch videos on **YouTube**.
10. Can you send me a **text message** with your address?
11. I surf the **Internet** for fun and also to find useful information.
12. I check my **e-mail** every morning.

More to Teach:

Synonyms

take pictures	take shots	take snaps	snap photos
text message	text	message	
laptop computer	laptop	notebook	notebook computer
copy machine	copier	photocopier	photocopy machine

Brand Names Used as *Verbs*

Brand	Verb	Definition
Google	google	look for information using Google
Twitter	tweet	send a message on Twitter
Skype	skype	make a video call on the Internet

I don't know the answer. You should **google** it.

He **tweets** four or five times every day.

Helen **skypes** her sister in London every week.

Usage Note

We usually talk about pictures, text, and videos as being **on** the Internet. Likewise, when people are members of a website, they are also **on** it.

The video is **on** YouTube.

Are you **on** Facebook?

1. What websites do you visit every day?
2. How has technology changed since you were young?
3. Which technology companies do you trust?

Listen Up

Task I *Listen and check the thing that is being talked about.* Track 11

Dialogue 1	Dialogue 2	Dialogue 3	Dialogue 4
☑ Facebook	☑ e-mail	☑ printer	☐ touch screen phone
☐ YouTube	☐ text message	☐ MP3 player	☑ laptop computer

Task II *Listen again and complete the sentences with the words you hear.*

1. Brad has his **pictures** from Saturday's **party** on the Internet.
2. Marvin needs the **notes** for **history** class.
3. David can buy some **paper** for Matt.
4. Jenny has to **type** up her **homework**.

Act It Out

Practice the conversations with the expressions.

How often do you . . .
go online?
play video games?
check your e-mail?
watch videos on YouTube?
post pictures on Facebook?
look up information on Wikipedia?

Response
I . . . every day / week / weekend.
I . . . once / twice / three times / four times a day.
I never . . .
I . . . all the time / once in a while.

Did You Know...?

least often				most often
never	seldom rarely	sometimes once in a while	usually often	always all the time

1. Max exercises. (rarely) ▶ Max rarely exercises.
2. My father drinks coffee. (usually) ▶ My father usually drinks coffee.
3. Steve meets his friends. (once in a while) ▶ Steve meets his friends once in a while.
4. It is too late to quit smoking. (never) ▶ It is never too late to quit smoking.
5. I use Google to search for things online. (every day) ▶ I use Google to search for things online every day.
6. Do you go to the movies? (often) ▶ Do you often go to the movies?

Teaching Resources

Audio Transcripts for *Listen Up*: Track 11

Dialogue 1:

Brad: Hey, Jason. Look at my profile page. I have some **pictures** from Saturday's **party** there.

Jason: That's cool, Brad. Do you have a picture of Stacey there?

Brad: Yeah. She looks very good in it.

Dialogue 2:

Marvin: Hi, Stan. Can you send me the **notes** for **history** class? My address is marv@mail2.com.

Stan: Sure, Marvin. I can send them to you right now.

Dialogue 3:

David: Can you help me, Matt? I need to print something.

Matt: I'm sorry, David. There isn't any **paper**.

David: That's not a problem. I can buy some for you.

Dialogue 4:

Mom: You should do your **homework**.

Jenny: I'm almost finished. I just need to **type** it up.

More to Teach:

Position of Adverbs of Frequency

Before *main verbs*	He **usually** eats dinner with Susan.
After *be* verbs	Anne is **never** late. She's **always** on time.
After *modal verbs*	You can **always** visit me anytime.
At the start or end of the sentence (for emphasis)	**Sometimes** I walk to school.

Usage Note

1. Adverbs of frequency come before ***be* verbs** in short answers.
   A: Is Sandra **usually** nice to people?
   B: Yes, she **usually** is.
2. We usually don't put **always** at the beginning or end of the sentence.
3. If the adverb of frequency is a longer phrase, we normally put it at the end of the sentence.
   We go to the beach with our parents **every few weeks**.

Conversation

Homework or Video Games?

Listen and fill in the blanks with the word choices given. Track 12

sometimes	anymore	send	losing	seldom	chat

Steve is playing a video game. Sandra comes up to say hello.

Sandra: Hi, Steve. What are you doing? Do you want to meet tonight? We can go to dinner and do homework together.

Steve: Oh no! I am 1. **losing** this game! What? Oh. Hi, Sandra. How's it going?

Sandra: You're always playing with your toys. We never talk 2. **anymore**!

Steve: That's not true. We 3. **chat** all the time. We are talking right now.

Sandra: You prefer posting on Facebook to meeting your friends.

Steve: I meet my friends 4. **sometimes**. I can also see what they are doing on their Facebook page.

Sandra: And what about reading books? You 5. **seldom** read. You need to do it more often.

Steve: Reading is boring. I prefer video games to reading.

Sandra: Fine. Well, would you like to meet later? I can help you with homework.

Steve: Sorry, I can't. I have to 6. **send** a lot of e-mails tonight.

Sandra: You should send them now! You are behaving like a little boy.

Key Words

❶ anymore *adv.*

I can make my own decisions. I'm not a child anymore.

EXTENSION **Usage Note:**

> **Not . . . anymore** and **not . . . any longer** can both be used to show that something was true in the past but is not true now.
>
> He was on the school basketball team in college, but he doesn't play anymore.
>
> (He was on the school basketball team in college, but he doesn't play any longer.)

❷ chat *v., n.*

I like to chat with my classmates after school.

We need to have a chat with Fred.

EXTENSION **Usage Note:**

> **Chat** is very informal and gives the idea that two people are talking. **Talk** can be used for one person. **Speak** is a little more formal than **talk. Say** is used for quoting speech.
>
> Miriam often **talks** to me about her family.
>
> You should **speak** to the boss about the problem.
>
> He **says** that he is fine.

❸ all the time *phr.*

synonyms: the whole time, very often

My father works all the time. I never see him.

EXTENSION **Other Phrases with *Time*:**

Phrase	Definition	Example
at times from time to time	sometimes	At times, he's very friendly to me.
at all times	always	You must stay inside at all times during an earthquake.

❹ post *v.*

He posts pictures on the website every day.

EXTENSION **Other Usage of *Post*:**

Harriet has a great post in the company. (means *a job*).

Key Words

❺ **page** *n.*

The Web page is mainly about sports.

❻ **boring** *adj.* | synonyms | dull, uninteresting |

This show is boring. Let's turn off the TV.

EXTENSION **Usage Note:**

Do not confuse **boring** with **bored** (*adj.* feels uninterested) or **bore** (*v.* make someone feel uninterested). Compare the examples below:

Charlie is really **boring**. He talks about clothes all the time.

I'm really **bored**. I don't like listening to Charlie.

Charlie **bores** me. I don't want to hear about clothes anymore.

❼ **behave** *v.* | synonym | act |

Tina behaves badly in class. Her parents are really worried about her.

EXTENSION **behavior** *n.*

His behavior makes his teacher very angry.

A. Complete the Passage

Use the word choices given to complete the passage.

meet	lose	chat	prefer	post	behave

Do you 1. **chat** on the Internet every day? Do you 2. **post** on Facebook when you are in class? Do you 3. **prefer** surfing the Net to going out? Do you feel sad when you 4. **lose** a game on the computer? Then you have a problem. You should not 5. **behave** like that. Go outside more often. 6. **Meet** your friends in a coffee shop or play sports. Who knows? You might enjoy yourself more.

B. Adverbs of Frequency

Fill in the blanks with the words given. More than one answer is possible in some of the sentences.

always	never	all the time	sometimes	seldom	often

Dialogue 1

Brad: How **often** do you buy new clothes, Todd?
Todd: I **never/seldom** buy new clothes. They're too expensive.
Brad: Really? So what do you do when your clothes get old?
Todd: **Sometimes** my parents buy me new clothes for my birthday.

Dialogue 2

Donna: I love this new TV show. It's called *Big Family*.
Karen: I don't know that show. I **never/seldom** watch TV at night.
Donna: I watch TV **often/all the time**. I love it.
Karen: TV is OK. But I like to chat with my friends. That's **always** fun.

C. Language Tips

Making Suggestions

You / We need to + Verb.	Why don't you / we + Verb?
You / We should + Verb.	Why not + Verb?

Practice stating problems and giving suggestions.

Problem	Suggestion
• The schoolwork is difficult.	• Ask your teacher for help.
• I think I'm sick.	• Go to see a doctor.
• My phone doesn't work.	• Call the phone company.
• I can't find room 102.	• Look at the school map.
• I feel tired.	• Get some sleep.

Present Continuous Tense

Statements

Subject	Be Verb	(Not)	Verb + –ing
I	am	(not)	watching the news on TV.
Derek	is	(not)	dancing to the music.
The children	are	(not)	having breakfast.

Questions

Question	Response
Is Mr. Lee having a meeting now?	Yes, he is. / No, he isn't.
Are the dogs sleeping?	Yes, they are. / No, they aren't.
What are you doing?	I'm writing an e-mail to my friend.
Where is Bob's mother going?	She is going to the grocery store.

Verb + –ing

Verb Ending	The –ing Form	Example	
one vowel + one consonant	repeat the consonant, then add **–ing**	running	hitting
one vowel + one consonant + **–e**	drop **–e**, then add **–ing**	coming	leaving
others	add **–ing**	reading	singing

Usage

We use the **present continuous** to talk about situations below.

now	We are talking right now.
repeated action (often negative)	You're always playing with your toys.
around the present time	Maggie is studying hard for her exams this week.
future events	I'm going out tomorrow.

Common time expressions

now	around the present time	in the near future
(just) now right now at the moment	today this week this month	tomorrow on Saturday next week

Grammar Practice

A. Complete the Letter

Write the correct articles tense of the verb. Add a ***be verb*** *if necessary.*

Dear Grandma,

It 1. **is raining** (rain) now, so I have time to write to you. I have to be quiet because Mom 2. **is sleeping** (sleep). I hear that you are sick. I 3. **hope** (hope) you feel better.

We 4. **are having** (have) a great time on our vacation. We 5. **are staying** (stay) in a nice hotel. It has a swimming pool. Tomorrow we 6. **are going** (go) to an amusement park. I really 7. **like** (like) amusement parks. Dad 8. **is taking** (take) lots of pictures with his new camera. See you soon!

Love,

Jennifer

B. Match

Listen and match the question with the response. Track 13

b 1. What is David doing right now?
d 2. Is David watching a cartoon?
c 3. Who is the hero fighting?
e 4. What is Neil doing later?
a 5. Who is having a birthday party tonight?
f 6. What is Ted always doing?

a. David's grandmother.
b. He is watching TV with his brothers.
c. He is fighting some bad guys.
d. No. He is watching an action movie.
e. He is going to the movies.
f. He is exercising all the time.

C. True or False

Listen and check ***True*** *of* ***False****.* Track 14

	True	False
1. They are fixing the cafeteria.	☐	☑
2. The chess club is looking for new members.	☑	☐
3. French club members are selling cookies.	☑	☐
4. The French club is going to Paris this year.	☐	☑
5. The football team is playing on Friday.	☑	☐
6. Buses for the football game are leaving at 4:00.	☐	☑
7. The Bible club is collecting old books for Ethiopia.	☐	☑
8. Mr. Vickers is getting married today.	☐	☑

Teaching Resources

Audio Transcripts for *Grammar Practice*:

B. Match Track 13

Neil: Hi, David. It's Neil. What are you doing right now?

David: Not much. I'm watching TV with my brothers.

Neil: What are you watching? Is it good?

David: It's just an action movie. Right now, the hero is fighting some bad guys.

Neil: What are you doing later? I'm going to the movies. The new Harry Potter movie is playing.

David: I can't go tonight. I'm going to my grandmother's birthday party. She's 70 today.

Neil: That's great. Wish her a happy birthday for me. Hey, what is Ted doing?

David: I think he's at the gym. He's always exercising.

Neil: That's true.

David: Listen, I have to get off the phone now.

Neil: OK. Enjoy the birthday party. Talk to you tomorrow.

C. True or False Track 14

Attention students. The restrooms on the second floor are not working. We are fixing the problem now. The chess club is looking for new members. You can join in the cafeteria during lunch. The French club needs money for their school trip. Members are selling cookies in front of the school. This year, they are going to Montréal, so help them out. Our school football team is playing Lakewood High on Friday. Buses are leaving from the front gate at 3:00. Come out and support the team. The Bible club is collecting old clothes for Ethiopia. Bring your old clothes to room 206. Finally, Mr. Vickers is getting married next week. We all wish him a happy marriage. Thank you.

Reading

Before You Read

Who are these people? Do you ever watch their videos? Where can you watch them?

It's a YouTube World

Track 15

In 2005, three friends: Steve Chen, Chad Hurley, and Jawad Karim created YouTube. Today, it is the biggest video website in the world. Anybody can post videos on it and have an opportunity to become famous. Justin Bieber is a great example. He was a regular teenager from a poor family in Canada. In 2008, his mother put his singing video on YouTube. A producer saw it and he really liked it. He decided to help Justin record an album. Now, Justin Bieber is a superstar thanks to YouTube. The site lets people visit places far away. They can sit at home and watch a video of an African dance group or a Brazilian soccer player. YouTube is more than just a website. It's a video universe!

While You Read

1. What country is Justin Bieber from?

2. Why does the writer call YouTube a "video universe?"

Interesting Facts about YouTube

- Justin Bieber's *Baby* has 402,051,105 views on YouTube around the world.
- 70 percent of users come from outside the U.S.
- You would need more than 1,000 years to watch all the videos on YouTube.

Key Words

❶ **opportunity** *n.*

The boss gave him an opportunity to go to China on business.

EXTENSION **Usage Note:**

> **Opportunity** and **chance** have the same meaning in many situations. **Opportunity** is used for something planned or given by a person. **Chance** is more random; it is related to luck.
>
> If you buy a ticket, you have a chance to win the prize.

❷ **famous** *adj.* | synonym | well-known |

That singer is very famous in Germany.

EXTENSION **fame** *n.*

Lots of people go to Hollywood to seek fame.

❸ **regular** *adj.* | synonym | ordinary |

Regular people don't have helicopters.

EXTENSION **Other Usages of *Regular*:**

I need to get regular exercise to become healthy. (means *happening very often*)

Peter usually orders a regular soda at lunch. (means *normal size*)

❹ **teenager** *n.*

Marcia is 12 now. She's nearly a teenager.

❺ **producer** *n.*

My uncle is a film producer. He makes horror movies.

❻ **decide** *v.*

It's a small company. The boss decides everything.

❼ **record** *v.*

I record the class on my phone and listen to it later.

EXTENSION **Other Usages of *Record*:**

We don't have a record of your call. (means *a document or note*)

He has the world record for the hundred meters. (means *the best ever*)

❽ **thanks to** *phr.*

Thanks to Jerry, we have enough money for the computer.

❾ **universe** *n.*

The universe is estimated to be 13,700,000,000 years old.

A. Word Definitions

Use the clues to fill in the blanks with the word choices given.

create	post	opportunity	famous	teenager	decide	album	superstar

1. My cousin knows a lot about the Internet. He can even **create** a website. (make)
2. He is the most **famous** movie star in Canada right now. (known about by many people)
3. Joe needs to buy Jessica a gift. Can you help him **decide** what to get? (make a choice)
4. My brother is a little younger than me. He's a(n) **teenager**. (someone between 13 and 19 years old)
5. Mary loves Lady Gaga. She wants to buy her latest **album**. (music CD)
6. Can you **post** the pictures from the wedding on Facebook? (put online)
7. I am meeting Kate for coffee. It's a great **opportunity** to ask her out. (chance)
8. This girl has a lot of talent. She could become a(n) **superstar**. (very popular person)

B. Words in Context

Choose the answers.

1. Anna is a classmate and good / bad friend. I **like** everyone in my class, including her.
2. He is like / not like everyone else. He's a **regular** person.
3. The **producer** directs / sings the production of the music album.
4. Justin is **recording** some songs / programs in the studio. He has a nice voice.
5. Jim is a happy / sad person **thanks to** his wife. She always supports him.

C. Multiple Choice

Circle the answers.

1. Why did a producer help Justin Bieber become famous?
   a. Because Justin's mother asked him to help.
   (b.) Because he liked Justin's singing on a YouTube video.
   c. Because he lived in the same neighborhood.
   d. Because Justin was already a superstar.

2. What does Justin Bieber's success prove?
   a. He is a very poor teenager from Canada.
   b. His mother thought he is poor at singing.
   (c.) Regular people can become famous thanks to YouTube.
   d. YouTube is the biggest website in the world.

3. Who can post videos on YouTube?
   a. Any person
   b. Justin Bieber
   c. African dance groups
   (d.) All the answers are correct.

4. What is NOT true about YouTube?
   a. Anybody can become famous through YouTube.
   (b.) Only managers can post videos on YouTube.
   c. People can watch videos from far away places.
   d. People can watch the worldwide news at home.

Looking Good

ANSWER KEY Student's Book ▶ p. 32

Words & Expressions

Listen and fill in the blanks with the descriptive adjectives below. Track 16

straight	slender	chubby	blonde	beautiful	dark
bald	curly	young	fit	short	slim

Physical Appearance

Photo 1

The 1. **young** girl is an actress. She has long 2. **blonde** hair. Her hair is 3. **straight**, not curly. She has 4. **beautiful** blue eyes. She is 5. **slender**.

Photo 2

The man doesn't have hair; he is 6. **bald**. He has 7. **dark** eyes. He is not fat; he is strong and 8. **slim**. He is old, but he still plays tennis.

Photo 3

This guy is not tall; he's 9. **short**. He's also 10. **chubby** because he rarely exercises. His eyes and hair are brown.

Photo 4

The woman has 11. **curly** hair. It is long and brown. She likes to exercise, so she is very 12. **fit**.

Practice

Put the descriptive adjectives from above in the appropriate columns.

Height	Build	Hair	Eyes	Age
tall **short**	**slender** **fat** **strong** **slim** **chubby** **fit**	**long** **blonde** **straight** **curly** **bald** **brown**	**beautiful** **blue** **dark** **brown**	**young** **old**

Teaching Resources

Audio Transcripts for *Words & Expressions*: Track 16

Photo 1: This woman has long **blonde** hair. Her hair is **straight**. The woman is very **young**. She is still a teenager. Her eyes are blue and **beautiful**. She is **slender**.

Photo 2: This man is **bald**. He has **dark** eyes. He is strong and **slim**.

Photo 3: This guy is **short**. He is also **chubby**. He has brown hair and brown eyes.

Photo 4: This woman is a runner. She jogs every morning to stay **fit**. She has long **curly** brown hair.

More to Teach:

Words that Mean *Thin*

Slim and **slender** can be used interchangeably to describe a thin person. Both **slim** and **slender** have positive connotations. **Thin** can be either positive or negative. **Skinny** also means "very thin," but in an unattractive way.

For Example:

Wendell is **slim** and healthy.

Ellen has a **slender** body.

You're very **skinny**. You should eat more.

Words that Mean *Not Tall*

Average height is the same as **normal height. Short** is used for saying someone is not very tall. **Little** often describes young children. It can mean "small and cute." **Tiny** means "very small."

For Example:

I'm **average height**, but my brother is quite **short**.

There's a **little** girl on the road.

Darren is **tiny**. He's only 150 centimeters tall!

Words that Mean *Fat*

Fat is OK to use about oneself, but we shouldn't use it about other people. **Overweight** is more polite. We often use **chubby** to say children are heavy. **Big** can mean "large," "strong," or "fat."

For Example:

I'm really **fat**. I shouldn't eat snacks between meals.

Harriet is a little **overweight**.

Do you see the **chubby** kid over there?

It's not easy for **big** men to find good clothes.

1. Can you name some beautiful people?
2. Do you want to look younger or older?
3. What is the first thing you notice about a person?

ANSWER KEY Student's Book ▶ p. 33

Listen Up

Task I *Listen and circle the correct pictures.* Track 17

Meet Sam's Family

Grandfather	Mother	Sister
ⓐ	ⓐ	a
b	b	ⓑ

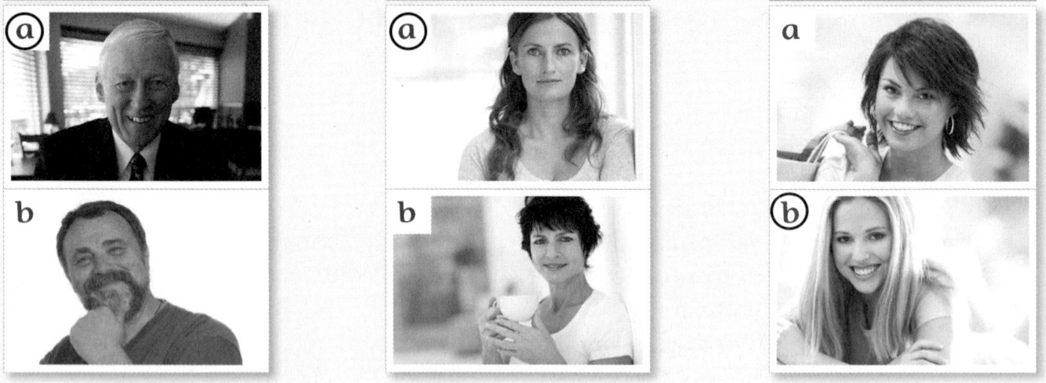

Task II *Listen again and fill in the blanks with the words you hear.*

1. Sam's grandfather has gray **hair**. He isn't **bald**.
2. Sam's mother is tall and **slim**. She also has long **brown** hair.
3. Sam has a(n) **younger** sister. Her eyes are **blue**, and her hair is long and **blonde**.

Act It Out

Bring a photo of a member of your family. Practice conversation using the word choices given.

grandma	grandpa	mom	dad	(elder / younger) brother	
(elder / younger) sister	cousin	short	tall	cute	slender
chubby	good-looking	curly hair	a beard	dark skin	black eyes

1. Is this your **grandma/grandpa/mom/dad/(elder/younger) brother/(elder/younger) sister/cousin**?
2. What's his / her name?
3. Is he / she a **short/tall/cute/slender/chubby/good-looking** person?
4. Does your **grandma/grandpa/mom/dad/(elder/younger) brother/ (elder/younger) sister/cousin** have **curly hair/a beard/dark skin/black eyes**?

Did You Know...?

Can you guess which sentence is more polite?	Polite	Impolite
1. There's Holly. She's **slender**.	☑	☐
Wow! Holly is so **skinny**.	☐	☑
2. John and I are in the same class. He's **fat**.	☐	☑
My classmate John is a little **chubby** / **overweight**.	☑	☐

Teaching Resources

Audio Transcripts for *Listen Up*: Track 17

This is my grandfather. He is old, but he is not **bald**. He still has **hair**. It is gray. He is tall and thin. He has blue eyes. He is a nice man.

I like this picture of my mother. She is **slim** and tall. Her hair is long and **brown**. She has big eyes and fair skin.

I have one **younger** sister. This is a picture of her. She has long **blonde** hair and **blue** eyes. She always says she is fat, but I think she is slender and beautiful.

More to Teach:

Adverbs of Degree

These adverbs are often used to modify descriptive adjectives.

Adverb	Example
a little	Jacob is a little short.
a bit	He's a bit younger than I am.
quite	Rachel's eyes are quite big.
pretty	Ian's hair is pretty curly.
almost	Ben is almost bald.
really	Jenny is really tall.

Usage Note

We can soften a negative adjective with phrases like **a little** or **a bit**. We often do this to make a statement more polite.

For Example:

He is **a little** skinny.

Diana is **a bit** loud.

Conversation

A Trip Home

Listen and fill in the blanks with the word choices given. Track 18

straight	country	chance	overweight	work	accountant

Liza and Jared talk outside the classroom.

Liza: Hey, Jared. What's up?

Jared: I flew home last weekend. It was a great trip.

Liza: You went back to your home 1. **country**? No way! I forget. Where are you from again?

Jared: I'm from New Zealand. I don't get to see my family often.

Liza: Then you were lucky to spend time with them. What do they look like?

Jared: My dad is tall, bald, and a little 2. **overweight**. My mom is slender, with 3. **straight** black hair. She's really beautiful. My younger sister, Jill, is chubby and cute.

Liza: I want to meet them sometime! What do your mom and dad do for 4. **work**?

Jared: My mother is a(n) 5. **accountant**. She loves working with numbers. My father is a computer engineer. He finds electronics interesting.

Liza: Cool. I'm happy that you got the 6. **chance** to return home.

Jared: Thanks. I miss my family already even though I love college.

Key Words

❶ **fly** *v.*

Carlos is nervous about flying, so he usually takes the train.

EXTENSION **Other Usage of *Fly*:**

Pilots spend around two years learning to fly. (means *control a plane*)

❷ **trip** *n.*

The first prize is a trip to Thailand.

EXTENSION **Usage Note:**

> **Travel** is the idea of going from place to place. **Journey** describes traveling from one place to another, usually over a long distance. A **trip** is a short return journey.
> **Travel** is good for your mind.
> The **journey** to Milan takes over 12 hours.
> I took a **trip** to the countryside last weekend.

❸ **No way!** *phr.* | synonyms | Really?; Wow!; I'm surprised. |

You got a new job so quickly? No way!

EXTENSION **Usage Note:**

> No way can also mean "it's not possible" or "I don't want to."
> **A:** Can we buy some food before we get on the train?
> **B:** No way. There isn't enough time.
>
> **A:** Do you want to see that movie?
> **B:** No way. My friends say it's terrible.

❹ **lucky** *adj.* | synonym | fortunate |

Jim is really lucky. He won $500 last week.

❺ **overweight** *adj.*

Both of my younger brothers are overweight. They eat too much fried food.

❻ **straight** *adj., adv.*

Paul has very straight teeth.

Drive straight ahead. The hospital is on the corner of Fifth Avenue and Park Street.

EXTENSION **Other Usage of *Straight*:**

Please be straight with me. I want to know the truth. (means *honest*)

❼ **miss** *v.*

Helen lives far away from home. She misses her family.

EXTENSION **Other Usages of *Miss*:**

Don't miss your train. Go to the station early. (means *be too late for*)

Ask Tom to help you check the information. He doesn't miss anything. (means *not notice*)

A. Antonyms

Match the word in bold with its antonym.

lucky	thin
spend	chubby
tall	curly
overweight	unfortunate
slender	short
straight	dull
interesting	save

B. Fill in the Blanks

*Use the correct form of the words in bold from **A** to complete the sentences.*

1. I **spent** my summer in Bali. I had a really good time.
2. My brother's hair isn't curly. It's **straight**.
3. Ted wasn't **lucky**. He missed his train.
4. My dog is **overweight**, now she needs to go on a diet.
5. Ed's new job sounds **interesting**. He meets many people from different countries.

C. Meanings in Context

Choose the meaning of the sentence in the conversation.

1. No way!
- **a.** That's too bad!
- (**b.**) That's great!

2. I don't get to see my family often.
- (**a.**) I don't usually have many opportunities to see my family.
- **b.** I don't like to see my family often.

3. He finds electronics interesting.
- **a.** He looks for interesting electronics.
- (**b.**) He enjoys learning about electronics.

4. I miss my family already even though I love college.
- (**a.**) I think of my family a lot.
- **b.** I forgot about my family.

D. Language Tips

Countries and Nationalities

Question		
Where are you from?	Where do you come from?	What's your nationality?
Response		
I'm from . . . / I come from . . .	I'm a(n) . . . / I'm . . .	I was born in . . .

Country	Nationality	Country	Nationality
The U.S. / America	American	The U.K. / England	Briton
Germany	German	Netherlands	Dutch
France	French	Turkey	Turkish

Simple Past Tense

Be Verbs

Statements

Subject	Past Tense of Be Verb	Sentence
I / He / She / It	was / was not (wasn't)	the winner of the race.
We / You / They	were / were not (weren't)	happy for the news.

Questions

Question	Response
Was Jessica the best player on the team?	Yes, she was. / No, she wasn't.
Why were Bob and his friend late to the party?	Because they were at work.
When was the play?	It was last Saturday.

Verbs

Verb Ending	Simple Past Form	Example	
–e	add –**d**	lived	arrived
one vowel + one consonant	repeat the consonant, then add –**ed**	stopped	begged
consonant + –**y**	change –**y** to –**ied**	tried	carried
others	add –**ed**	enjoyed	worked

Statements

Affirmative	Negative
I flew home last weekend. Kelly threw the ball to her dog. They lived in Los Angeles two years ago.	It didn't rain yesterday morning. Jamal didn't buy the expensive watch. My friends didn't like this band before.

Questions

Question	Answer
Did your brothers go to the gym this morning?	Yes, they did. / No, they didn't.
What did Iris buy yesterday?	She bought a beautiful necklace.
Who drank the milk on the table?	Molly did.

A. Complete the Passage

Use the correct form of the verbs in parentheses to complete the passage.

Travel Journal

My trip to Hawaii 1. **was** (be) great. I 2. **went** (go) for a week last summer. We 3. **flew** (fly) from San Francisco to Honolulu. Our plane 4. **arrived** (arrive) in the afternoon. We 5. **slept** (sleep) for a few hours at the hotel first. Then we 6. **watched** (watch) the sunset on the beach. The pictures from that day 7. **are** (be) now on my bedroom wall. The next day, I 8. **swam** (swim) in the ocean. Turtles 9. **were** (be) all around me. A few days later, we 10. **fished** (fish) in the ocean. I 11. **caught** (catch) a big fish. I really 12. **love** (love) Hawaii. I want to 13. **spend** (spend) another week there next year.

B. Match

Listen and match the question with the response. Track 19

e 1. Was Darren's accident inside the city?

c 2. Where was the hospital?

b 3. When was the accident?

a 4. Whom did Darren want to visit when he got in the accident?

f 5. What body part did Darren get hurt?

d 6. Why did Darren run into the car?

a. He wanted to see his friend Terry.

b. It was last Saturday.

c. It was near Darren's house.

d. He rode too fast, and the car turned in front of him.

e. No. It was outside the city.

f. He hurt his arm.

C. Correct the Mistakes

Fix the errors in the passage.

Many photographers go to Taroko National Park in Taiwan on August fifth every year to take pictures. What makes them go there? A long time ago, a photographer ~~take~~ took a picture there. The photographer's name ~~be~~ **was** Alison Wen. Wen's photo ~~be~~ **was/is** in black and white, not color. In the photo, you can see the moon near some mountains. It is beautiful and mysterious. It ~~become~~ **became** very popular. People see the picture and go to the same place to take the same picture just like Wen's. Scientists ~~studyed~~ **studied** the photo and ~~did say~~ **said** Wen ~~taking~~ **took** the picture of the moon around 7 o'clock in the evening. And every seven years, the moon ~~being~~ **is** in the same place over the mountains.

Teaching Resources

Audio Transcripts for *Grammar Practice*: Track 19

B. Match

Darren: I got into a bicycle accident.

Emily: Oh no, Darren! Are you alright?

Darren: I'm OK. My arm hurts a little though.

Emily: What happened? Did you see a doctor?

Darren: Ha-ha. Calm down! I'm fine. I rode too fast. A car turned in front of me, and I ran into it. I went to the hospital, but I wasn't hurt very much.

Emily: When did this happen?

Darren: It was last Saturday night. I was on my way to my friend Terry's house.

Emily: Was it in the city?

Darren: It was outside the city, about five minutes from my house. I was lucky because there was a hospital nearby.

Emily: Well, be more careful next time.

Reading

Before You Read

Do you think these women are beautiful? What do you think about these women's make up?

Dangerous Beauty

Track 20

While You Read

1. Why did women in Shakespeare's time shave the hair from their front hairlines and eyebrows?

2. What did people of the time think of as "perfect beauty?"

Can you imagine what fashions were like in Shakespeare's time? Believe it or not, pictures from his time show women who don't have eyebrows. They thought a high forehead was attractive and they shaved the hair from their front hairlines and eyebrows. Also many women dyed their hair red. At that time, women followed the style of Queen Elizabeth. Her red hair was a real vogue among women. In addition, a pale complexion was popular then. People thought of pale skin as a sign of nobility and delicacy. They used ceruse to whiten their faces. They applied this white foundation to their neck and chest, too. After making their skin white, they used a variety of reds upon their cheeks and lips. By doing this, women could get perfect beauty.

However the beauty they earned cost them dearly. Ceruse is a mixture of vinegar and lead powder, which is dangerous to their health. The lead poisoned them. Isn't it unbelievable that people would do anything to be beautiful?

Key Words

❶ **dangerous** *adj.*

Ice climbing is a dangerous sport but it is exciting.

❷ **attractive** *adj.* | synonym | charming |

The island has an attractive resort so many people visit there every year.

❸ **shave** *v.*

He cut himself while he was shaving this morning.

❹ **dye** *n., v.*

Ken colored his old shirt using a blue dye.
Angela dyed her hair blonde and it looks good on her.

❺ **follow** *v.*

Suddenly, she felt somebody was following close behind her.

EXTENSION **Other Usage of *Follow*:**
The story of the movie is too complicated to follow.

❻ **vogue** *n.*

The song had a great vogue in its day.

❼ **among** *prep.*

He is the best writer among English poets at that time.

❽ **delicacy** *n.* | synonym | grace, elegance |

The sculpture was carved with great delicacy.

❾ **poison** *n., v.*

Some mushrooms have a deadly poison.
Someone poisoned the food and killed the king.

❿ **beautiful** *adj.*

Seattle was more beautiful than I had thought.

EXTENSION **beauty** *n.*
She was the winner in the beauty contest last year.

A. Synonyms

Match the word in bold with its synonym.

imagine	guess
picture	portrait
many	numerous
dye	tint
unbelievable	impressive
vogue	trend

B. Fill in the Blanks

Use the words in bold from ***A*** *to complete the sentences. Change the word form if necessary.*

1. Henna likes to draw **pictures** of people walking on the street.
2. Old pop music has come back into **vogue** after the concert.
3. My sister **dyed** her hair green two years ago.
4. I can't **imagine** how angry you are.
5. It was **unbelievable** that all the people were gathering at the hall to see him.
6. I have **many** things to do, but I don't know what to do first.

C. Words with Different Meanings

Match the word in bold with its definition.

1 Her **face** turned red with shame when everyone looked at her. **(a)**
How can I **face** her? We haven't seen each other for years after we fought. **(b)**
Definition: (a) *n.* the front part of the head (b) *v.* to meet or confront

2 If you want to **apply** for this job, you need a Bachelor's degree in nursing. **(b)**
It is effective to **apply** mayonnaise to your hair as a conditioner. **(a)**
Definition: (a) *v.* to spread (b) *v.* to request formally

3 Even small amounts of **lead** can cause serious health problems. **(a)**
He can inspire the members and **lead** the team to victory. **(b)**
Definition: (a) *n.* a heavy toxic metallic element (b) *v.* to guide or control

D. True or False

Check ***True*** *or* ***False.***

	True	False
1. Queen Elizabeth had red hair and most women in her time hated it.	☐	☑
2. Women changed their hair to black during the Elizabethan Era.	☐	☑
3. Women in Shakespeare's time shaved their eyebrows for beauty.	☑	☐
4. Lead is a cosmetic which is good for health.	☐	☑
5. Some women took a lot of risks in order to look beautiful.	☑	☐

NOTES

ANSWER KEY Student's Book ▶ p. 40

Not Feeling So Good

Words & Expressions

Fill in the blanks using the word choices given.

cough	runny nose	toothache	headache	fever
stomachache	sore throat	neck pain	sleeping problems	

Symptoms

1

I have a **fever**.

8
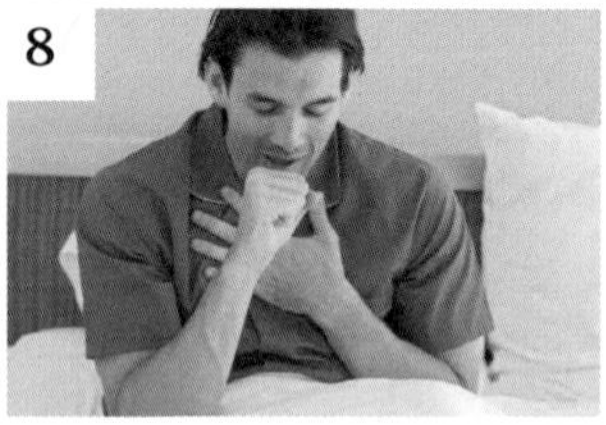
I have a **cough**.

2

I have a **headache**.

4
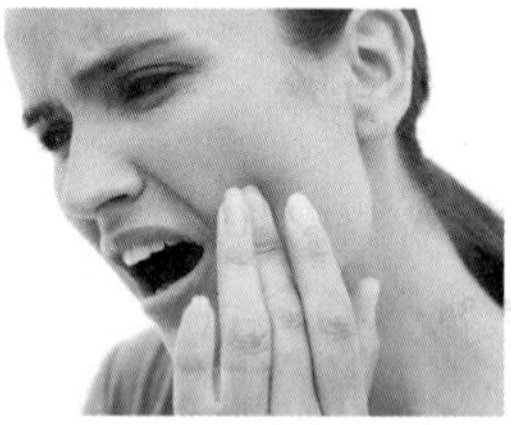
I have a **toothache**.

7

I have a **sore throat**.

3

I have a **runny nose**.

6

I have a **stomachache**.

5

I have a **sleeping problems**.

9
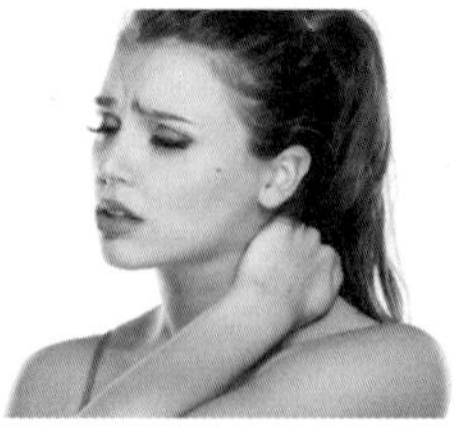
I have a **neck pain**.

Listen and write the correct sentence number in the box. Track 21

Practice

Talk to a partner.

- How often do you go to see a doctor?
- Have you ever had a high fever?
- What do you do to keep healthy?

Teaching Resources

Audio Transcripts for *Words & Expressions*: Track 21

1. Joe's body temperature is 40 degrees Celsius.
2. My head hurts a lot.
3. You should wipe your nose. Here's a handkerchief.
4. Michelle needs to see a dentist.
5. Susan only sleeps two hours a night. She feels very tired.
6. I think I ate something bad today.
7. I can't speak. My throat hurts too much.
8. Cover your mouth! I don't want to get sick too.
9. My neck hurts. I can't move my head.

More to Teach:

Alternative Sentences

I have a fever.	=	I have a high temperature.
I have a cough.	=	I cough a lot.
I have a headache.	=	My head hurts.
I have a toothache.	=	My tooth is killing me.
I have a sore throat.	=	My throat is sore.
I have a runny nose.	=	My nose is running.
I have a stomachache.	=	I have a pain in my stomach.
I have sleeping problems.	=	I have problems sleeping.
I have neck pain.	=	My neck is bothering me.

1. Do you go to see a doctor every time you feel unwell?
2. What foods do you eat when you are sick?

Listen Up

*Listen and check **True** or **False**.* Track 22

Sally didn't go to work today.	True	False
1. She was out in the rain.	☑	☐
2. Her head hurts.	☑	☐
3. She has a toothache.	☐	☑
4. She thinks she has a stomachache.	☐	☑
5. She needs to rest at home.	☑	☐

Johnny is sick. His dad is very worried.	True	False
1. His stomach hurts a lot.	☑	☐
2. He feels dizzy.	☑	☐
3. He doesn't want any food.	☑	☐
4. He has a high fever.	☐	☑
5. The pain makes him cry.	☑	☐

Act It Out

Practice the conversations with the word choices given.

dizzy	sick	tired	weak	bad
headache	sore throat	neck pain	sore muscles	
head	throat	neck	muscles	

1. **A:** I feel **dizzy/sick/tired/weak/bad**.
   B: Do you have (a) **headache/sore throat/neck pain/sore muscles**?
   A: Yes, I do. My **head/throat/neck/muscles** hurt(s) a lot.
2. **A:** My **head/throat/neck/muscles** is / are sore.
   B: Really? Me too! I also have (a) **headache/sore throat/neck pain/sore muscles**.
3. **A:** Would this medicine help my **headache/sore throat/neck pain/sore muscles**?
   B: No, but it can help your **sore throat/neck pain/sore muscles/headache**.

Did You Know...?

There are different ways to talk about pain.

head ear back tooth stomach	I have a(n) **head**ache.
throat neck feet back muscles	I have (a) sore **throat**. My **back** is / are sore. My **neck** is / are hurting. My **feet** hurt(s).

Teaching Resources

Audio Transcripts for *Listen Up*: Track 22

Sally Gets Sick

I left my umbrella at home yesterday. It rained hard. My clothes were completely wet. Today, I feel really bad. I have a sore throat and a runny nose. My head hurts too. I can't get out of bed. I think I have a fever. I should check my temperature. I need to rest for a few days.

Johnny Gets Sick

Doctor, my son is sick. He can't go to school. He has a stomachache. Sometimes the pain makes him cry. He feels very weak. He said he feels dizzy sometimes. It's hard for him to walk. He doesn't want to eat anything. He can only drink water. His tongue is yellow. I think this is serious. Help him, doctor!

More to Teach:

Different Usages of *Hurt*

Part of Speech	Usage	Example
verb	to injure	I fell and **hurt** my hand.
verb	to make one feel pain	This cut really **hurts**.
verb	to make someone feel sad	Don't talk like that. It **hurts** Darren.
adjective	physically or emotionally injured	He was badly **hurt** in the accident. He feels **hurt** because you didn't call him.

Usage Note

Pain vs. Ache vs. Sore

Pain is usually a *noun*, used for physical or emotional suffering. It can also be used to describe a person or situation that causes you inconvenience. **Ache** is either a *noun* or *verb*. It's used for longer-lasting pain. **Sore** is an *adjective* and is usually used for muscles.

For Example:

The bus is really full in the morning. It's a real **pain**.

After James played tennis, he had an **ache** in his hand.

I hurt my shoulder last week. It still **aches**.

My lower leg is very **sore**. I ran too much yesterday.

Feeling Sick?

Listen and fill in the blanks with the word choices given. Track 23

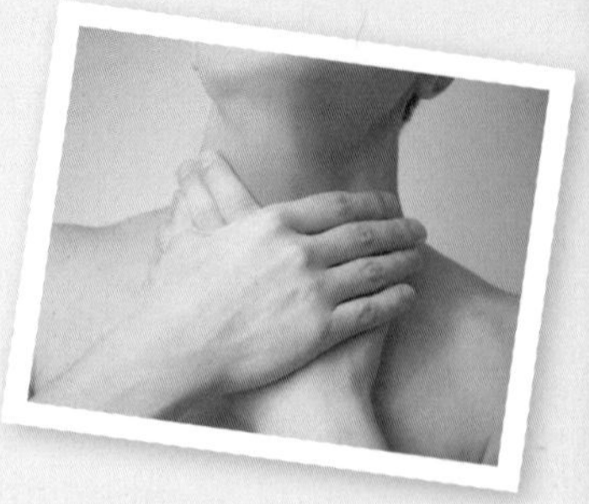

sore	deeply	fever	possible	pill	take

Nick is talking to a nurse on the phone.

Nick: Hello. I'd like to see Dr. Chan as soon as 1. **possible** .

Nurse: Can I 2. **take** your name?

Nick: My name's Nicholas Wang.

Nurse: Dr. Chan has time this afternoon. Would you be able to come in at three o'clock?

Nick: That sounds fine. Thanks.

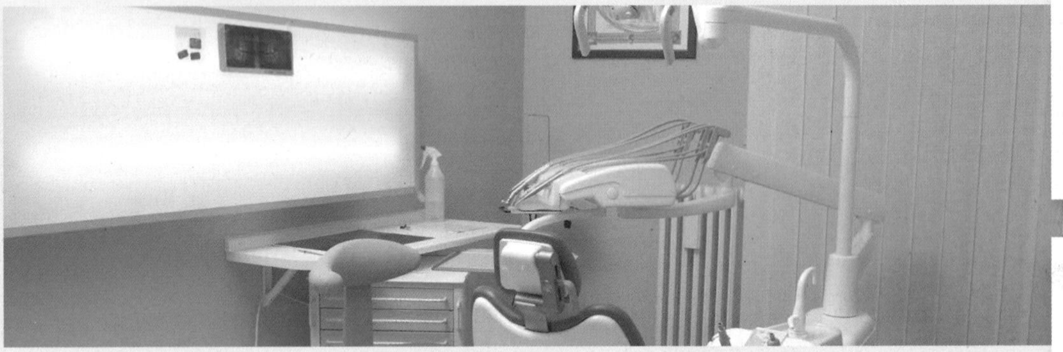

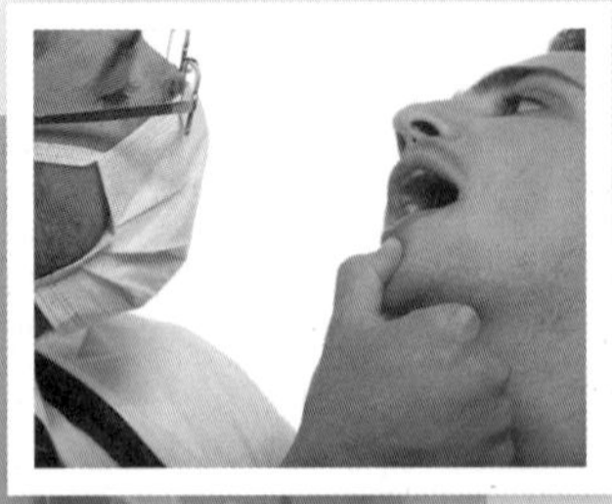

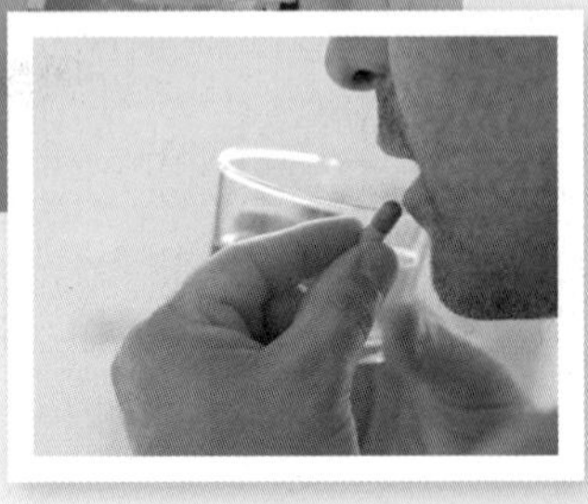

(Nick enters the doctor's office.)

Dr. Chan: Hi, Nick. What's the matter?

Nick: I have a high 3. **fever** and a headache.

Dr. Chan: Does your body hurt?

Nick: Yes. My neck hurts, and my muscles are 4. **sore** . And I can't stop coughing.

Dr. Chan: When did the pain start?

Nick: I started feeling bad last week. My mom made me take out the garbage. It was cold outside. I was sick a day later.

Dr. Chan: Can I have you take off your shirt? Now breathe 5. **deeply** . Hmm. It doesn't sound good. Let me check your throat. It looks red. Are you taking any medicine at the moment?

Nick: No.

Dr. Chan: OK. Please take this medicine with food. It can make you feel better. Take one 6. **pill** every six hours and drink lots of water.

Nick: Thank you.

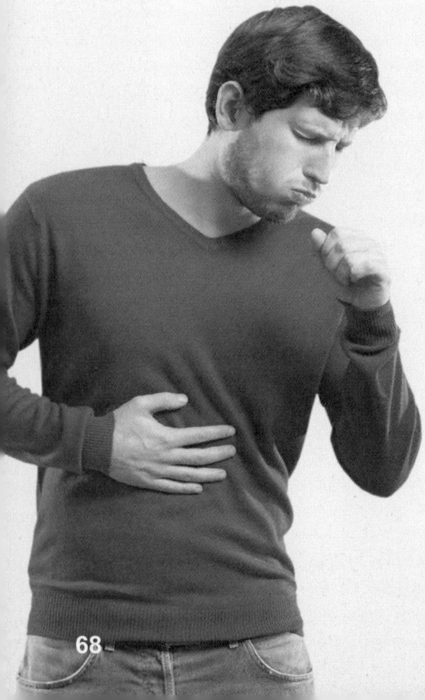

Key Words

❶ **as soon as possible** *phr.* synonym | as soon as one can

Please get back to me as soon as possible.

❷ **take** *v.*

I usually take notes in class.

EXTENSION **Other Usages of *Take*:**

Remember to take your medicine before bedtime. (means *swallow*)

You should take your father's advice and study law. (means *accept*)

Learning a language takes a lot of effort. (means *need*)

❸ **be able to** *phr.*

I live far from here, so I'm not able to start work so early.

EXTENSION **Usage Note:**

> **Be able to** can mean "have time to do something" or "have the skill to do something." Compare the examples below:
> I'm not able to pick you up from the airport. My car broke down.
> Tina is able to manage her time well. She always finishes her work on time.

❹ **fever** *n.*

I need to take my daughter to the hospital. She is running a fever.

EXTENSION **Other Usage of *Fever*:**

Everyone in America has football fever during the Super Bowl.

❺ **can't stop + Verb + -ing** *phr.* (used for continuing something you don't want to)

My eyes are sore. I can't stop rubbing them.

❻ **cough** *n., v.*

I have the flu. I keep coughing all day.

Honey is helpful when you have a cough.

❼ **take off** *phr.*

He took his boots off before he entered the house.

EXTENSION **Other Usages of *Take Off*:**

I feel nervous when the plane takes off and lands. (means *rise into the air*)

Nancy is sick. She needs to take today off. (means *not go to work or school*)

❽ **breathe** *v.*

When you feel scared, try to breathe deeply.

EXTENSION **breath** *n.*

It's so cold. I can see my breath in the air.

A. Word Definitions

Use the clues to fill in the blanks with the word choices given. Change the word form if necessary.

be able to	fever	take off	breathe	at the moment	lots of

1. Tom **is able to** come to my party. He doesn't have to work on that day. (can)
2. I'm not too busy **at the moment**. (right now)
3. Feel Johnny's forehead. He seems to have a **fever**. (temperature)
4. The house costs **lots of** money. (a large amount of)
5. Air pollution is serious in Beijing. It is hard to **breathe** outside. (take air into your lungs)
6. It's warm today. You should **take off** your jacket. (remove)

B. You Might Also Say . . .

Write the sentence from the conversation with the same meaning.

1. I want to see Dr. Chan very soon.
   = **I'd like to see Dr. Chan as soon as possible.**
2. May I have your name?
   = **Can I take your name?**
3. Do you have any pain?
   = **Does your body hurt?**
4. I keep coughing as well.
   = **And I can't stop coughing.**
5. Please don't take this medicine on an empty stomach.
   = **Please take this medicine with food.**

C. Language Tips

Making an Appointment

A Patient Might Say . . .	A Nurse Might Say . . .
I'd like to see Dr. (last name) (time).	Dr. (last name) has time (time).
I need to see a doctor (time).	Would you be able to come in (time)?
Could I come in (time)?	When would you be available to come in?
Can Dr. (last name) see me (time)?	When would you like to come in?
Does Dr. (last name) have time to see me (time)?	How about (time)? / Is (time) possible?

Practice the sentence patterns using the information given.

The patient is available...	on Wednesday morning	today between 1 and 4	right now
The doctor is available...	at 11 on Tuesday	after two on Friday	today at 2:30

ANSWER KEY Student's Book ▶ p. 44

Linking Verbs

Definition

Most verbs are action verbs. They tell what the subject does. Some verbs link an adjective or a noun to the subject. We call them **linking verbs.**

be	feel	look	taste	smell	sound
appear	seem	become	grow	turn	remain

Mr. Chan is a good doctor.
I feel sick.
Your throat looks red.

Usage

Some linking verbs can be used in more than one way. Action verbs are usually used with **adverbs,** not **adjectives.**

Example	Verb Usage	Meaning
The noodles tasted good.	linking verb	to have a taste
I tasted the noodles.	action verb	to eat

Example	Verb Usage	Meaning
The leaves turn yellow in fall.	linking verb	to change
The road turns sharply.	action verb	to curve

Causative Verbs

A **causative verb** is used when someone causes something to happen.

Verb	Structure	Meaning
make	make + somebody + Verb	to cause one to do something
have	have + somebody + Verb	to order one to do something
let	let + somebody + Verb	to allow one to do something
get	get + somebody + to Verb	to ask one to do something

My mom made me take out the garbage.
Can I have you take off your shirt?
Let me check your throat.
I got Clara to send you some information.

A. Recognize Linking and Action Verbs

*Decide if the word in bold is a **linking verb** or an **action verb**. Check the box.*

	Sentence	Linking Verb	Action Verb
1	Eddie **looked** at his sister.		✓
	You **look** tired.	✓	
2	People start to have health problems when they **grow** older.	✓	
	This plant **grows** well in most areas.		✓
3	The dog **smelled** the food.		✓
	That white flower **smells** sweet.	✓	
4	The man **sounded** the alarm.		✓
	Your mother called me. She **sounded** worried.	✓	

B. Words in Context

Choose the answers.

1. The man **turned** the pages of the book slow / slowly.
2. You should try to **remain** calm / calmly during an emergency.
3. When Molly thinks of her grandma, she **becomes** sad / sadly.
4. A man **appeared** sudden / suddenly at my door.
5. This meat **tastes** bad / badly. We should throw it away.
6. I **feel** tired / tiredly. I need to get some rest.
7. Kathy **seems** happy / happily at her new job.
8. My hair **grows** quick / quickly. I need to get a haircut every month.

C. Fill in the Blanks

*Use the words **make**, **have**, **let**, or **get** to complete the sentences. Change the word form if necessary. For some questions, more than one answer is correct.*

1. Can you __**get**__ your brother to help me?
2. My parents don't __**let**__ me go out at night.
3. Can you __**have**__ your secretary send me the letter?
4. Dr. Linda __**made/had**__ her students correct their mistakes last class.
5. Please __**get**__ John to drive me to school.
6. Ben is a funny person. He always __**makes**__ me laugh.
7. __**Let**__ me take a look at your work.
8. Mrs. Kelly __**has/had/makes/made**__ her son clean his room.

Worksheet

Task I

Use the correct form of the verbs to complete the sentences. Some blanks may have more than one correct answer.

be	look	smell	taste	turn	become	remain	sound

1. The food ______________ good. I can't wait to try it.
2. Kenny ______________ tired of fast food. He wanted to have a healthy diet.
3. My skin ______________ brown every summer.
4. Did you hear that? It ______________ like a dog.
5. That dress ______________ great on you.
6. I drank some nice tea this morning. It ______________ like lemon.
7. Mark ______________ angry when Tara is late.
8. There is a small fire. Please ______________ calm and walk toward the exit.

Task II

Correct the mistakes.

1. I made him to go to bed for an hour.
   → ____
2. The weather turned coldly last week.
   → ____
3. He seemed more happily after eating.
   → ____
4. My brother lets me to wear his clothes sometimes.
   → ____
5. There seems to be a problem with my car. I can't get it start.
   → ____
6. Alex's boss had him worked on weekends.
   → ____
7. We should get Chris buy us some food when he goes to the store.
   → ____
8. The teacher made her students writing a story about their best friends.
   → ____

This page may be photocopied and distributed to the class.

Reading

Before You Read

Look at the pictures. When do we need these things? Which one do you think is the most useful?

Natural Medicine for Your Cold

Track 24

While You Read

1. How is garlic helpful?

2. What food is good for a runny nose?

3. When should you use honey?

When you get sick, what do you do? Some people go to the drugstore to buy medicine. Some visit the doctor, and some just rest at home.

Some foods can make you feel better when you're sick. Most people know that green tea improves your health when you have a cold. Strawberries help when you have the flu, and honey is good if you have a sore throat.

Did you know that garlic is also effective? Garlic can prevent colds. It also makes them last for a shorter time. Just don't forget to brush your teeth after you eat it!

Hot peppers are also effective. Spicy peppers help stop a runny nose. Of course, you don't need to eat the peppers by themselves. You can mix them with your food.

Chicken soup is another cold remedy. Some doctors started recommending chicken soup as a cold medicine back in the 12th century. The chemicals in chicken soup are similar to those in modern medicine.

The next time you're coughing, sneezing, or fighting a fever, don't go to the drugstore. Try some healthy foods instead!

Key Words

❶ **natural** *adj.*

Fruit is a healthy natural snack.

❷ **drugstore** *n.* synonym | pharmacy

Coca-Cola was first sold in a drugstore.

❸ **rest** *v., n.*

I need to take some time off work and rest for a few days.

Henry looks tired. He should get some rest.

EXTENSION **Other Usage of *Rest*:**

You can eat the rest of the pie if you want. (means *what is left*)

❹ **effective** *adj.*

That plan was effective. We finished the job very quickly.

❺ **prevent** *v.*

You should warm up before you exercise. It can prevent injuries.

EXTENSION **prevention** *n.*

Crime prevention is the police's job.

❻ **last** *v.*

The rainy weather lasted for a whole week.

EXTENSION **Other Usages of *Last*:**

I always eat my favorite part of the meal last. (*adv.* after all others)

I started working here last August. (*adj.* most recent)

❼ **remedy** *n.* synonym | cure

Ginger tea is a good remedy for colds.

❽ **recommend** *v.*

Can you recommend a good restaurant near here?

EXTENSION **Usage Note:**

Recommend is used in three patterns:

recommend something to someone	Joe recommended a band to me.
recommend that someone do something	I recommend that you take a bus tour of the city.
recommend doing something	The hotel is very popular. They recommend booking early.

❾ **sneeze** *v., n.*

Jeff just sneezed. It was really loud!

You can hold your nose to stop a sneeze.

A. Word Definitions

Use the clues to fill in the blanks with the word choices given. Change the word form if necessary.

natural	drugstore	prevent	effective	flu	sore	recommend	century

1. Drinking green tea could **prevent** cancer. (stop)
2. I have a high fever. Maybe I have the **flu**. (illness similar to a bad cold)
3. There is a(n) **drugstore** around the corner. You can buy cold medicine there. (shop selling medicine)
4. It took 97 years – almost a(n) **century** – to finish the building. (100 years)
5. Tim knows a(n) **effective** way of losing weight. He lost 20 pounds in one week. (successful)
6. This yogurt is completely **natural**. It's made from milk and fresh fruit. (not made by people)
7. Laura ran 12 kilometers yesterday. Her legs are really **sore** now. (painful)
8. Seth **recommended** this movie to me. I hope it's good. (suggest)

B. Words with Different Meanings

Match the word in bold with its definition.

1 I hurt my ankle, so I need to **rest** for a few weeks. ⓑ
You can have the **rest** of my French fries. I'm full. ⓐ
Definition: ⓐ *n.* what is left ⓑ *v.* to stop activity

2 What's the **last** movie you went to see? ⓐ
Lunar New Year celebrations **last** for 15 days. ⓑ
Definition: ⓐ *adj.* most recent ⓑ *v.* to continue for a period of time

3 The whole country had soccer **fever** during the World Cup. ⓐ
Charles was in bed all day with a high **fever**. ⓑ
Definition: ⓐ *n.* a kind of excitement ⓑ *n.* a high body temperature

C. Complete the Passage

Use the correct form of the words given to complete the passage.

brush	remedy	fight

Bad breath can cause a lot of problems. It might make it difficult for you to find a boyfriend or girlfriend or to advance in your career. There are several kinds of 1. **remedies** for bad breath. One is keeping your mouth clean by 2. **brushing** your tongue. Another way to 3. **fight** bad breath is to drink lots of water. These solutions not only help bad breath, but they can also make a cold go away.

NOTES

The Big Screen

Words & Expressions

Write the movie type under each poster.

a romance movie	a horror movie	a western	a drama
a comedy	a science-fiction movie	an action movie	a cartoon

Types of Movies

4

an action movie

2

a horror movie

5

a comedy

6

a science-fiction movie

7

a drama

1

a cartoon

8

a romance movie

3

a western

Listen and write the sentence number in the box. Track 25

Practice

Talk to a partner.

- What is your favorite movie type?
- What kind of movies don't you like?
- How often do you watch movies?
- Do you prefer to watch movies at a movie theater or at home?

Teaching Resources

Audio Transcripts for *Words & Expressions*: Track 25

1. Filmmakers used drawings and computers for this movie.
2. Today is Halloween. Let's watch a really scary movie tonight!
3. These movies are about the Wild West in 19th century America.
4. This movie is exciting. The police try to catch some bank robbers.
5. I like to laugh. Are there any funny movies playing at the theater?
6. I want to see a movie about scientists controlling people's brains.
7. These movies try to show people's real emotions.
8. It's about two young lovers. It's a great movie for a date.

More to Teach:

Genres

Many words used for types of movies can also be used for types of books and TV shows. Look at the examples below:

Movie	Book	TV Show
science-fiction (sci-fi)	sci-fi book	sci-fi show
comedy	X	sitcom
horror (movie)	horror story	horror show
romance (movie)	romance (novel)	romantic soap opera
western	western	western TV series
action (movie)	X	action TV series
cartoon	comic	cartoon

More on Types of Movies

a historical movie	an animated movie	an independent movie
a war movie	a musical	a sports movie
a romantic comedy (a rom-com)	a documentary movie	an art movie

1. What are your favorite movies?
2. Are there any types of movies that you don't like?
3. How often do you go to the movies?

Listen Up

Task I *Listen and check the box.* Track 26

	Statement	*Dead Earth*	*The Bad Cook*
1	The children are unhappy because their parents fight all the time.	✓	
2	The character opens a restaurant.		✓
3	The character hides from the police.		✓
4	The husband tries to find his wife.	✓	
5	People got sick after eating at the restaurant.		✓

Task II *Listen again and fill in the chart.*

Movie	Type	Description	Good Actors?	Good Movie?
Dead Earth	a drama	silly, (sad), scary, bad, (serious), (intelligent)	☑ Yes ☐ No	☑ Yes ☐ No
The Bad Cook	a comedy	excellent, (dumb), funny, (boring), strange, (horrible)	☐ Yes ☑ No	☐ Yes ☑ No

Act It Out

Practice the conversation with the word choices given.

serious exciting scary romantic
drama(s) action movie(s)
horror movie(s) romance movie(s)
like it too don't like it
never saw it want to see it
actor actress director

1. A: I like serious/exciting/scary/romantic movies.
   B: Me too. I prefer to watch dramas/action movies/horror movies/romance movies.
2. A: This is a great movie. It's a(n) drama/action movie/horror movie/romance movie.
   B: I like it too/don't like it/never saw it/want to see it.
3. A: My favorite actor/actress/director is (*name*).
   B: I agree. I enjoy his / her dramas/action movies/horror movies/romance movies.

Did You Know...?

see a movie	star in a movie	make a movie
go to a movie	appear in a movie	shoot a movie
go to the movies	be in a movie	
take in a movie		

Use the phrases above to complete the sentences. Change the word form if necessary.

1. The director made/is making/shot/is shooting a/the movie in Venice, Italy.
2. What are you doing on Friday night? Do you want to see a movie/go to a movie/go to the movies/take in a movie?
3. My uncle isn't a famous actor, but he starred/appeared/was in a movie 20 years ago.

Teaching Resources

Audio Transcripts for *Listen Up*: Track 26

Dead Earth

The movie *Dead Earth* is a drama about a married couple. They have two children. They fight a lot. This makes the children unhappy. One day, the wife disappears and the husband tries to find her. This movie studies the character of the wife. The main actress is Julia Richards. She is excellent. This movie is serious and sad. It also has an intelligent plot. This is a great movie!

The Bad Cook

The movie *The Bad Cook* is about Jonathan. Jonathan is a college student. One day, he decides to open a restaurant, but he can't cook. A few customers get sick. The police want to arrest Jonathan, so he tries to hide from them. This is a comedy, but the jokes are dumb. The story is horrible. It's also a pretty boring movie. The main actor is very bad. You should watch something else. Don't waste your time and money!

More to Teach:

Movie Vocabulary

Word	Definition	Example
A-list	the best	*The Departed* has **A-list** actors, such as Leonardo DiCaprio and Matt Damon.
box office	movie theater	The movie did well at the **box office**. It made a lot of money.
role	a character in a movie	John Travolta is excellent in his **role** as the bad guy.
cast	all the actors and actresses in a film	The **cast** includes Colin Farrell and Jamie Foxx.
hit	successful	Adam Sandler is always in **hit** movies. All my friends go to see them.

Conversation

Movie Night

Listen and fill in the blanks with the word choices given. Track 27

waiting	comedy	third	angry	forgive	agreed

Jeff and Jordan are waiting by the movie theater. Jessica comes by.

Jeff: Well, Jessica is late.

Jordan: This is the 1. **third** time this month!

Jeff: She is never on time. We 2. **agreed** to meet at half past seven. It's ten to eight now!

Jessica: Guys . . . Hi. I'm late. I'm really sorry.

Jeff: Come on, Jessica. This is not the first time. You came late to John's party on Friday.

Jessica: Please don't be 3. **angry** at me.

Jordan: It's alright. Don't worry about it.

Jessica: Thanks for 4. **waiting**. The popcorn is my treat tonight.

Jeff: I love popcorn! OK. We 5. **forgive** you. I'm excited about this movie!

Jessica: Who's in it?

Jeff: Will Smith and that British girl. I forgot her name.

Jessica: What is it about?

Jeff: It's a(n) 6. **comedy** about two friends. I heard it's really funny.

Jordan: The movie opened in the first week of April. All my friends saw it already.

Jeff: The movie starts in five minutes. Jessica, you still have enough time to buy us popcorn and drinks.

Jessica: Drinks too? OK, I guess. Let's go in.

Key Words

❶ come by *phr.*

He was reading in the park when his friend came by.

EXTENSION **Other Usages of *Come By*:**

If you come by my house later, I can lend you the book. (means *make a short visit*)

Jobs are difficult to come by these days. (means *get*)

❷ on time *phr.*

You should always be on time for class.

EXTENSION **Usage Note:**

> **On time** means "at the planned time." **In time** means "with time left."
> I got to their house in time. They were still there.

❸ agree *v.*

I don't agree with Molly. I think she's wrong.

EXTENSION **agreement** *n.*

Your father and I are in agreement. You must study harder!

❹ come on *phr.*

Come on, Peter. Don't lie to us.

EXTENSION **Other Usages of *Come On*:**

Come on! We only have five minutes to get there. (means *hurry*)

Come on, Tigers! You can do it! (used to encourage someone or a team)

❺ angry *adj.*

A lot of things make Kevin angry. He is always shouting.

EXTENSION **Usage Note:**

> We say we are **angry at** or **with** someone, but **angry about** or **over** something.
> I'm **angry at** / **with** Jim. He borrowed money and didn't pay me back.
> Jerry is really **angry about** / **over** the decision.

anger *n.*

There's a lot of anger in your voice. What's the matter?

Key Words

❻ treat *n.*

Let's try the new French restaurant. It's my treat.

EXTENSION **Other Usages of *Treat*:**

Bob took his son to Disney as a birthday treat. (*n.* a gift)

She treats her pet cat like one of the family. (*v.* deal with)

The doctor used a new kind of medicine to treat the patient. (*v.* try to cure)

❼ excited *adj.*

The kids are very excited. It's Christmas Day tomorrow.

EXTENSION **Usage Note:**

> To **excite** is to cause someone to be emotional. **Exciting** is an *adjective* for something that excites people.
> The idea really **excites** me. I want to know more.
> (That's an **exciting** idea. Tell me more.)

excitement *n.*

When the singer came onto the stage, it caused a lot of excitement.

A. Meanings in Context

Choose the meaning of the sentence in the conversation.

1. She is never on time. (**a.**) She is always late. **b.** She never knows the time.	**2.** Come on, Jessica. **a.** Come over here, Jessica. (**b.**) Don't make excuses, Jessica.
3. The popcorn is my treat tonight. (**a.**) I will buy you some popcorn. **b.** The popcorn tastes great tonight.	**4.** The movie opened in the first week of April. **a.** The movie played in theaters for one week in April. (**b.**) The movie started playing in theaters in April.

B. Word Definitions

Use the clues to fill in the blanks with the word choices given.

agreed	guy	forgive	comedy	funny	enough

1. I'm really sorry. I hope you can **forgive** me someday. (not be angry anymore)
2. This is my favorite movie. It's really **funny**. (makes people laugh)
3. Jessica and I decided to watch a movie. Tony **agreed** to join us for the movie. (say *yes*)
4. Look at that **guy** with a yellow hat and a big dog. (man)
5. I want to buy that book. Do we have **enough** money left? (amount you need)
6. Tom likes to see a(n) **comedy**. It makes him laugh. (humorous movie)

C. Fill in the Blanks

Use the prepositions in the box to complete the sentences. Some choices can be used more than once.

past	at	by	about	to

1. Could you come **by** my office this afternoon?
2. It's only 11:03. The bus leaves at half **past** eleven.
3. Samuel always comes early **to** class.
4. Tom closed the door violently because he was angry **at** his sister.
5. Don't worry **about** your test. You studied very hard.
6. Karen's son is excited **about** his birthday party.

D. Language Tips

Apologizing

Saying Sorry	Showing Anger	Forgiving
I'm really sorry.	Come on!	It's alright / OK.
Please don't be angry at / with me.	Give me a break!	Don't worry about it.
I apologize.	How could you do this?	We forgive you.
This is my fault.	I can't believe this!	It's not a big deal.

Talking about Time

Prepositions

Preposition	Usage		Example	
in	months seasons	years periods of time	in June in (the) winter	in 2025 in the first week of April
on	dates days of the week	holidays	on March 31st on Friday	on Christmas
at	clock time		at 3 p.m.	at half past seven

Questions

Question	Response
When is your vacation?	It is in August.
What day is Halloween?	It is on Thursday.
What time is our train?	It is at 10:20.
What time is it? / What is the time?	It / The time is three o'clock.

Usage Note

We can write dates as regular numbers, but must remember to say them as ordinal numbers (first, second, third, etc.). Use ordinal numbers for streets and the floors of buildings as well.

Telling Time

Use the following phrases to tell time.

0-30 minutes	(*minutes*) **past** / **after** (*hour*)	30 minutes	half **past** (*hour*)
15 minutes	(*a*) quarter **past** / **after** (*hour*)	31-60 minutes	(*minutes*) **to** (*hour*)

	It's seven oh five. It's five (minutes) **past** / **after** seven.		It's seven thirty. It's half **past** seven.
	It's seven fifteen. It's (a) quarter **past** / **after** seven.		It's seven forty-five. It's (a) quarter **to** eight.

A. Correct the Mistakes

Fix the errors in the passage.

My friend Jenny lives on ~~Six~~ **Sixth** Avenue. Her twenty-first birthday is ~~at~~ **in** two weeks. It's ~~in~~ **on** June 25th. Her birthday is ~~in~~ **on** Monday, but we are having a party ~~in~~ **on** the weekend.

Jenny likes sports very much. She gets up ~~on~~ **at** seven every ~~mornings~~ **morning** and exercises. ~~In~~ **At** noon, she eats a healthy lunch with lots of vegetables. She loves to run. She even ran a marathon ~~at~~ **in** 2009. ~~On~~ **In** summer, Jenny and I play tennis ~~in~~ **on** Thursday afternoons. She is really good and beats me most of the time. Last Thursday, however, I beat her!

B. Match

Listen and match the question with the response. Track 28

__c__ 1. When does the big sale begin?

__d__ 2. What day does the sale end?

__e__ 3. When are women's shoes 50 percent off?

__f__ 4. Are men's dress pants 40 percent off on Sunday?

__b__ 5. What time does the toy sale begin?

__a__ 6. When do the doors open from Monday to Friday?

a. They open at 9 a.m.

b. It begins at seven in the evening.

c. It starts on November fifth.

d. Sunday is the final day.

e. They are half price on Thursday.

f. No, but they are on Friday and Saturday.

C. Fill in the Blanks

Listen and write the words you hear to complete the sentences. Track 29

Hamilton Movie House Showtimes

Toy Adventure	3:10 p.m.	5:30 p.m.	7:50 p.m.	midnight
The Biggest Gun	1:00 p.m.	4:25 p.m.	9:45 p.m.	opened on August 18th
Where Am I?	4:30 p.m.	8:45 p.m.	11:35 p.m.	opens on August 22nd

1. Stephen and Carl enjoy going to the movies in __summer__ to stay out of the __heat__.
2. The first __showing__ of *Toy Adventure* is at __ten__ after __three__.
3. Stephen thinks *Toy Adventure* is a movie for __kids__.
4. The __action__ movie *The Biggest Gun* is showing at a(n) __quarter__ to __ten__, but Carl thinks it's too __late__.
5. Today is August __twentieth__; *Where Am I?* doesn't __open__ until the __twenty-second__.

Teaching Resources

Audio Transcripts for *Grammar Practice*:

B. Match Track 28

Welcome to the Hudson Bay Department Store. Don't miss our big sale. It starts on Wednesday, November fifth and lasts for five days. This branch opened in 1982. This is our store's biggest sale ever. On Thursday, all women's shoes are 50 percent off. That's right. 50 percent off! And all men's dress pants are 40 percent off on Friday and Saturday. All you kids, tell your parents about the special sale. All toys are 30 percent off after seven every evening. The doors open at nine a.m. on weekdays and ten a.m. on weekends. Come out and save!

C. Fill in the Blanks Track 29

Stephen: I love going to the movies in the **summer**.

Carl: Me too. It's great to get out of the **heat**. Do you want to see *Toy Adventure*? The first **showing** is at **ten** after **three**.

Stephen: That movie is for **kids**. I want to see *The Biggest Gun*. It's an **action** movie. There's a showing at 4:25.

Carl: It's also playing at a **quarter** to **ten**. That might be too **late** though. Do you know anything about *Where Am I?*

Stephen: It's a comedy about a guy traveling in Europe. That might be better. It stars Tom Hands. There's a showing at half past four. That's perfect.

Carl: Wait a minute. It **opens** on August **twenty-second**. Today's only the **twentieth**.

Stephen: I guess we have to see *The Biggest Gun*.

ANSWER KEY Student's Book ▶ p. 54

Before You Read

Look at the pictures. Do the animals below remind you of certain movies?

The Wildest Job in Movies

Track 30

While You Read

1. Who is Mark Forbes? What does he do?

2. How many types of animals are in Evan Almighty?

3. Why do animal actors have doubles?

There are dozens of jobs on a movie set, and some of them are a little strange. One of the most unusual jobs belongs to animal coordinators. These workers have to train and control all of the animals in a movie.

Coordinators have to manage more than one animal for a role. Like humans, almost all main animal characters have at least one double. The double must look just like the star. There might be one dog to do tricks, another to stay in one place, and a third to run from one place to another.

The animal coordinator for the movie *Evan Almighty*, Mark Forbes, had a huge challenge. He had to train about 100 types of animals to walk onto a large boat. He filmed many of the animals separately — he didn't want them to run after each other. After careful planning and effort, Forbes and his team managed to work to keep the animals healthy and maintain a safe atmosphere on the set. Managing animals on a movie set is a wild and unusual job. Do you want to try it?

More Unusual Jobs

- Greensmen place plants in film scenes.
- Armorers are responsible for the guns in a movie.

Key Words

❶ **wild** *adj.*

The crowd went wild when the band came on.

EXTENSION **Other Usages of *Wild*:**

There are lots of wild animals in the forest. (means *not being raised by humans*)

Mosquitoes are the most dangerous animal in the wild. (means *nature*)

---

❷ **dozens of** *phr.* synonym: a lot of

Dozens of people wanted to talk to Jake about his new book.

EXTENSION **a dozen** *phr.*

Could I have a dozen eggs, please? (means *12*)

---

❸ **coordinator** *n.*

Molly is a great coordinator. Everything is under control.

EXTENSION **coordinate** *v.*

The UN coordinated with the government to get food to the people.

---

❹ **trick** *n.*

His dog can stand on two legs. It's a cool trick.

EXTENSION **Other Usages of *Trick*:**

People play tricks on each other for fun on April Fool's Day. (means *a joke*)

I tricked him into doing my work for me. (means *fool*)

---

❺ **challenge** *n., v.*

The project is a challenge, but we can do it.

Mr. Thomas is a great professor. He likes to challenge his students to think.

---

❻ **separately** *adv.*

We paid separately. My sandwich was $2 and his was $2.50.

EXTENSION **separate** *v., adj.*

A river separates the two cities.

You should use separate knives to cut vegetables and meat.

---

❼ **maintain** *v.*

Gloria maintains her house well. It always looks good.

---

❽ **atmosphere** *n.*

The restaurant has a relaxing atmosphere.

A. Fill in the Blanks

Use the word choices given to complete the sentences. Change the word form if necessary.

set	film	role	character	double	scene

1. Rachel is playing a leading **role** in the movie.
2. The actor had two **doubles** to do the running and fighting for him.
3. The street is closed because people are **filming** a movie.
4. It was a very sad **scene**, and the audience began to cry.
5. The main **character** in the comedy is a young doctor.
6. It took six months to build the **set** for the movie.

B. Words in Context

Choose the answers.

1. **Dozens of** people bought tickets, so we prepared a few / a lot of chairs.
2. We decided to get a wedding **coordinator** to pay for / plan our wedding day.
3. The final exam was a **challenge**. It was very easy / hard for the students.
4. This set of books is sold **separately**. You can buy them one by one / together.
5. I like the **atmosphere** of my neighborhood. People can live in a safe environment / air.

C. Words with Different Meanings

Match the word in bold with its definition.

1. Ted **managed** his own store for two years. ⓐ
   Julia was tired, but she **managed** to finish the race. ⓑ
   Definition: ⓐ *v.* to handle or direct ⓑ *v.* to succeed in doing something difficult

2. My brother believes everything, so it's easy to **trick** him. ⓑ
   The elephants can do some **tricks**. ⓐ
   Definition: ⓐ *n.* a clever act to entertain ⓑ *v.* to fool someone

3. The mayor wants to **maintain** control of the city. The voters get to decide next week. ⓑ
   Dan didn't have a job, so his wife had to **maintain** the family. ⓐ
   Definition: ⓐ *v.* to support ⓑ *v.* to keep the same condition

D. True or False

*Check **True** or **False**.*

	True	False
1. Mark Forbes had to train animals to run after each other.	☐	☑
2. There were around 100 types of animals in *Evan Almighty*.	☑	☐
3. Mark Forbes filmed animals for *Evan Almighty* one by one.	☑	☐
4. In a movie with animals, a double looks just like another animal.	☑	☐
5. A safe atmosphere is important when animals are on the set.	☑	☐

ANSWER KEY Student's Book ▶ p. 56

How Do You Feel?

Words & Expressions

Listen and write the sentence number of the feeling in the box. Track 31

Feelings

1

happy

8

lonely

6

sad

3

proud

2

nervous

10

down

9

calm

5

mad

4

jealous

7

comfortable

11

curious

12

afraid

Practice

Talk to a partner. What makes you feel a certain way?

- **Reading this book** puts me in a good mood.
- **The rain** makes me feel sad.
- I get nervous when **giving a speech**.
- **This painting** makes me feel comfortable.

Teaching Resources

Audio Transcripts for *Words & Expressions*: Track 31

1. Joanne is very **happy**. She just won first prize at the piano contest.
2. Fiona feels **nervous** when she goes to the dentist.
3. Jenna got on to the cheerleading team. She is very **proud**.
4. Jane gets **jealous** when Jason talks to other girls.
5. Where is my file? I hate my computer! I'm so **mad**.
6. Nicole is **sad** because her parents are always fighting.
7. You are my best friend. I feel **comfortable** when I talk to you.
8. This dog looks **lonely**. Maybe I should bring him home.
9. I like listening to music. It makes me feel **calm**.
10. I am feeling **down**. I got some bad news in a text message.
11. Fred is **curious** about the present. He wants to open it now.
12. I'm really **afraid** of spiders! Take it away.

More to Teach:

Synonyms

Word	Synonym			
happy	glad	pleased	joyful	in a good mood
mad	angry			
sad	down	unhappy	upset	blue
afraid	scared			

Word Usage

1. Lonely vs. Alone

Being or feeling **lonely** is to feel sad because there's nobody around. Being **alone** means there are no other people there. It can be a good thing.

I felt **lonely** after my girlfriend left me.

I like to go fishing **alone**. It's very relaxing.

2. Calm as *Adjective* and *Verb*

adjective	not excited or angry
verb (often used with **down**)	to relax or to get someone to relax

Wesley is a very **calm** person. He is never upset.

I tried to **calm** Jerry **down**, but he's still shouting.

1. Do you usually feel good when you wake up?
2. What emotions have you felt today?
3. Do animals have emotions?

Listen Up

Task I *Listen and fill in the blanks with the words from* ***Words & Expressions.*** Track 32

1. Lucy is __**happy**__. She was accepted by a university in London.
2. Stacey is __**sad**__. James didn't call her today.
3. Jeff is __**nervous**__. He didn't study at all.
4. Alex is __**mad**__. He thinks Barbara is lying to him.

Task II *Listen again and check* ***True*** *or* ***False.***

	True	False
1. Lucy wants to study physics in London.	☐	☑
2. Lucy got a phone call from a school in England.	☐	☑
3. Stacey thinks James likes her a lot.	☐	☑
4. Jeff didn't study much for the exam.	☑	☐
5. Alex doesn't believe Barbara.	☑	☐

Act It Out

Practice the conversations with the word choices given. Change the word form if necessary.

exam	interview	baseball game	speech
happy	glad	sad	down
get a good grade	pass the driving test	receive bad news	fail the class

1. A: How was the __**exam/interview/baseball game/speech**__?
   B: It was good. I'm __**happy/glad**__. / It was terrible. I feel __**sad/down**__.
2. A: Did you __**get a good grade/pass the driving test/receive bad news/fail the class**__?
   B: Yes, I did. / No, I didn't. I'm very __**happy/glad/sad/down**__.
3. A: Did something happen? You look __**sad/down**__.
   B: Yeah, you're right. I'm really __**sad/down**__. I __**received bad news/failed the class**__.

Did You Know...?

Fill in the blanks with the prepositions below. Some choices can be used more than once.

for of about at

1. I'm afraid __**of**__ cockroaches.
2. Susan is nervous __**about**__ the speech.
3. I'm really happy __**for**__ Sam. He's getting married.
4. The woman is proud __**of**__ her children.
5. The people are mad __**at**__ the president.

Teaching Resources

Audio Transcripts for *Listen Up*: Track 32

Dialogue 1:

John: Hey, how is it going?

Lucy: Things are great! I just got a letter from a university in London. They accepted my application to study business there.

John: That's fantastic! Congratulations.

Lucy: Thank you! It's a dream come true.

Dialogue 2:

Rebecca: Why the long face, Stacey?

Stacey: I went on a date with James last night.

Rebecca: Did it not go well?

Stacey: I liked him, but he didn't **call** me today. I guess he doesn't want to go out again.

Rebecca: I'm sorry.

Dialogue 3:

Sara: Hi, Jeff. Are you smoking again?

Jeff: Yeah. I'm really nervous about the test tomorrow.

Sara: Don't worry. You're a smart guy.

Jeff: I didn't study at all today. I'm too nervous to study.

Sara: Why don't you go for a run?

Jeff: Great idea. But I don't have time. I need to study!

Dialogue 4:

Alex: Where is my cell phone? I can't find it! Barbara, did you touch my phone?

Barbara: No, I didn't touch your phone.

Alex: Well, where is it?

Barbara: How would I know?

Alex: Where could it be? It was right here a moment ago! Are you lying to me?

Conversation

Bad News, Good News

Listen and fill in the blanks with the word choices given. Track 33

bored	happened	better	marry	down	shocked

Jennifer and Stan meet for dinner.

Jennifer: Hey, Stan. Is everything OK? You look a little 1. **down**.

Stan: Everything is fine.

Jennifer: Look. We're friends. You can tell me. You shouldn't feel embarrassed about anything.

Stan: I guess you're right. Alright. Ashley broke up with me.

Jennifer: I'm so sorry. What 2. **happened**?

Stan: She didn't say. Maybe she was 3. **bored** with me. Am I a boring person?

Jennifer: No. You're very interesting. That's why I'm your friend.

Stan: I'm pretty 4. **shocked** about this. I didn't expect it at all.

Jennifer: She didn't express anything?

Stan: No. This is so confusing!

Jennifer: Keep your head up. You can find someone 5. **better**.

Stan: I'm not so sure. How about you? How are you doing?

Jennifer: Well . . . I have some news, but I can tell you later.

Stan: I thought we were friends.

Jennifer: Michael asked me to 6. **marry** him. I said *yes*.

Stan: Wow. Congratulations!

Jennifer: Are you sure you're OK?

Stan: Of course. I'm really happy for you.

Jennifer: Thanks, Stan. Let's go have a drink. You shouldn't be alone tonight.

Key Words

❶ **embarrassed** *adj.*

Peter walked into the girls' bathroom. He was really embarrassed!

EXTENSION **embarrassing** *adj.*

Singing in front of so many people is embarrassing.

embarrass *v.*

His mother loves to embarrass him. She makes him wear silly clothes.

❷ **break up (with someone)** *phr.* synonym split up (with someone)

Maria broke up with Arnold a few months ago.

❸ **sorry** *adj.*

The woman's husband died in an accident. I feel sorry for her.

EXTENSION **Other Usages of *Sorry*:**

I'm sorry for being late. The traffic was bad this morning. (used to apologize)

I'm sorry, but we don't have any rooms available right now. (used to introduce bad news)

❹ **shocked** *adj.*

Everyone was shocked by the terrible news.

EXTENSION **shock** *v., n.*

News of her death shocked everyone.

It was a shock when the boss said he would have to close the factory.

❺ **expect** *v.*

We expect to complete our work by the end of month.

❻ **express** *v.*

Cindy expressed an interest in studying law.

EXTENSION **Other Usages of *Express*:**

I gave him an express order. (*adj.* clear, definite)

The express is much quicker than the normal train. (*n.* a high-speed train)

❼ **marry** *v.*

Today, many people choose to marry late.

EXTENSION **married** *adj.*

Nick is married. He has three children.

marriage *n.*

I'm too young to think about marriage.

❽ **congratulations** *n.*

Congratulations on your success! Well done!

EXTENSION **congratulate** *v.*

I'd like to congratulate her on her new baby.

A. Synonyms

Match the word in bold with its synonym.

down	unhappy
boring	dull
shocked	surprised
express	say
alone	by yourself

B. Fill in the Blanks

*Use the words in bold from **A** to complete the sentences.*

1. It's difficult for me to **express** my feelings because I'm shy.
2. Uncle Lynn doesn't have a computer. It's so **boring** when I go to his house.
3. When she's **alone** at night, she feels afraid.
4. Sad songs always get me **down**.
5. Emma was **shocked** by the news. She didn't believe it.

C. Meanings in Context

Choose the meaning of the sentence in the conversation.

1. You shouldn't feel embarrassed about anything.
- (**a.**) You can share everything with me.
- **b.** You should hide your feelings.

2. Ashley broke up with me.
- **a.** Ashley broke some of my things.
- (**b.**) Ashley left me.

3. I'm so sorry.
- **a.** I made a mistake.
- (**b.**) I feel bad for you.

4. I didn't expect it at all.
- (**a.**) It was a big shock to me.
- **b.** I had a feeling about it.

5. Keep your head up.
- (**a.**) Try to think about good things.
- **b.** Don't look at the ground.

6. You shouldn't be alone tonight.
- **a.** You need more space.
- (**b.**) You need to be with a friend.

D. Language Tips

Asking about Someone's Feelings

In Negative Situations	In All Situations
Is everything OK / alright?	What happened?
What's wrong?	Why are you so (*emotion adjective*)?
Why the long face?	

Participial Adjectives

Usage

Present Participial Adjectives(–ing)	Past Participial Adjectives(–ed)
Present participials(-ing) are used to describe the causes of feelings. The book is boring.	Past participials(-ed) are used to describe feelings. I feel bored when I read the book.

Paired Adjectives

Verb	–ing Adjective	–ed Adjective
bore	boring	bored
embarrass	embarrassing	embarrassed
interest	interesting	interested
shock	shocking	shocked
confuse	confusing	confused
tire	tiring	tired
excite	exciting	excited
satisfy	satisfying	satisfied
frighten	frightening	frightened
worry	worrying	worried

The basketball game **excited** me.
I was **excited** by the basketball game.
I had fun at the basketball game because it was **exciting**.

Usage Note

Verb + -ing words and **-ing adjectives** look the same. Pay attention to how they are used.

For Example:
The dog is **frightening** the boy.
(the present continuous)

The dog is **frightening**.
(–ing adjective)

Past Participial Adjectives with Prepositions

Some past participials(-ed) are followed by a preposition and a noun.

be bored with	be tired of
be embarrassed about	be excited about
be interested in	be satisfied with
be shocked about / by	be frightened of
be confused by	be worried about

I'**m tired of** the weather. It always rains in Seattle.
She'**s** not **worried about** the test. She always does well in French.

A. Choose the Feeling

Write the best adjective given to describe each situation.

embarrassing	confusing	exciting	frightening	shocking	tiring	satisfying	worrying

1. We had a good meal in an Italian restaurant. **satisfying**
2. There are too many road signs. **confusing**
3. I ran in the park for two hours. **tiring**
4. I wore two different shoes to school today. **embarrassing**
5. Jay lost a lot of money. His financial situation isn't good. **worrying**
6. I never watch horror movies because they scare me. **frightening**
7. I can't believe it! Mr. Lee is leaving his wife for another woman! **shocking**
8. My heart beats fast when I jump out of an airplane. I love the feeling! **exciting**

B. Words in Context

Choose the answer.

1. Helen Keller **inspired** many people. Her story is inspired / inspiring.
2. Let's go to the beach and **relax**. Taking a rest at the beach is relaxed / relaxing.
3. I didn't want to **embarrass** you. Unfortunately, you look embarrassing / embarrassed.
4. This TV show **bores** me. The story is bored / boring.
5. Mr. Starr likes to **encourage** people. His students seem encouraged / encouraging to study more.
6. Modern art **interests** Vicky. She's interested / interesting in the topic.
7. Your dad **frightens** me. He's really frightened / frightening.
8. The news **pleases** me. I'm pleased / pleasing.

C. Correct the Mistakes

Fix the errors in the passage.

Most of us are ~~excite~~ excited by Leonardo DiCaprio's films. Movies such as *Titanic* and *The Beach* are popular and ~~interested~~ **interesting**. But he isn't ~~satisfy~~ **satisfied** with just acting. Leonardo is ~~shocking~~ **shocked** by the damage to the environment, so he works hard to save the earth. He's also worried ~~in~~ **about** wild animals. In 2010, he gave $1,000,000 to Russia to save its tigers. The Russian leader, Vladimir Putin, called him a "real man." But Leonardo ~~embarrassing~~ **was embarrassed** about this. We never get ~~tiring~~ **tired** of Leonardo DiCaprio's films. We're interested ~~with~~ **in** his kind acts as well.

Worksheet

Task I

Take a look at the chart. Choose the correct words.

An **–ing adjectives** tell us the *cause of an emotion*. An **–ed adjectives** tell us *how someone feels*.
For Example: The situation is **worrying**. I am really **worried** about it.

1. Walking for so long is very tired / tiring.
2. The boy was frightened / frightening when he saw the spider.
3. Those pictures of me are really embarrassed / embarrassing.
4. The question is too confused / confusing. I don't understand it.
5. Henry was shocked / shocking after he heard the news.
6. My dog gets excited / exciting if I pick up his food bowl.

Task II

Fill in the blanks with the correct prepositions.

1. A: Do you want to come to the football game later? **B:** No, thanks. I'm not really interested ________ football.	**2. A:** I have a date with Penny tonight. **B:** Are you excited ________ it?
3. A: Do you need help with the reading? **B:** Yes. I'm confused ________ this sentence.	**4. A:** Tell me that story again. **B:** No. I'm tired ________ telling the same story.
5. A: Are you satisfied ________ his answer? **B:** No. I'd like to ask him a few more questions.	**6. A:** Why did you move to the city, Tommy? **B:** I was just bored ________ life in the countryside.

This page may be photocopied and distributed to the class.

Reading

Before You Read

Look at the pictures. Do you think animals have feelings? Do they also have intelligence?

Do Animals Have Feelings?

Track 34

While You Read

1. What was René Descartes' opinion about animals and emotions?
2. Which animals are playful?
3. How are monkeys like humans?

To the famous philosopher René Descartes, only humans had emotions. Animals were just machines — they didn't have the ability to think. Today, there is a lot of evidence about animals' feelings.

Animals can feel more than basic emotions like the fear observed when they run away from danger. According to scientists, the moods of animals such as elephants, geese, and bears show a sharp change after a loved one dies. Penguins are the same way. In fact, two adult penguins at the London Zoo once stopped eating when their baby was stolen. Animals' emotions are more complex than previously thought. Dolphins and rats are as playful and cheerful as children. They are fun-loving animals. Baboons, a type of monkey, feel stress just like a human.

Some scientists still believe that animals have no feelings. They say that animals only act in certain ways to get a prize, such as food. Animals don't talk, so we can't be sure about their thoughts. What do you think? Do animals have emotions? If so, should humans treat them in a different way?

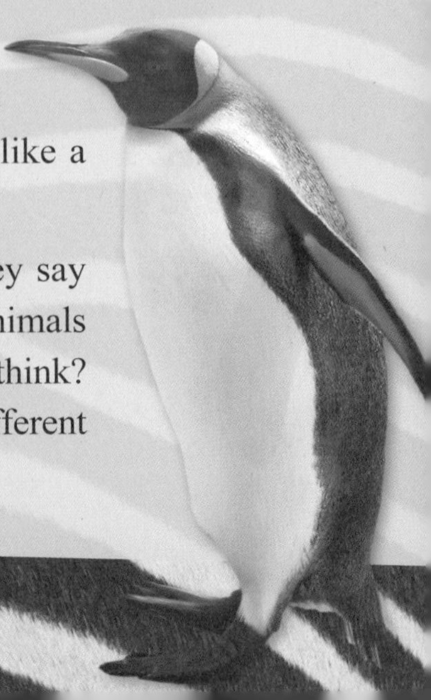

Key Words

❶ feeling *n.*

It's a great feeling to help people.

EXTENSION **Usage Note:**

> **Feeling** is a little more general than **emotion. Emotions** only cover states of mind; **feelings** cover both states of mind and physical feelings. For example, sadness is a feeling and an emotion, while pain is a feeling, but not an emotion.
> When Bill's cat died, he didn't show any emotion.

❷ ability *n.*

He has a great singing ability. He should be a singer.

EXTENSION **able** *adj.*

Mario is an able plumber. He can fix anything.

be able to *phr.*

I am not able to lift this box. It's too heavy.

❸ evidence *n.*

We think he took the money, but we don't have any evidence.

❹ basic *adj.*

I learned a few basic French words when I was in Paris.

❺ fear *n.*

Fear makes people do crazy things.

EXTENSION **Usage Note:**

> To **have a fear of** is the same as **be afraid of** or **be frightened of**.
> Many small children **have a fear of** going to the doctor.
> (Many small children **are afraid / frightened of** going to the doctor.)

❻ mood *n.*

Edwin is alone in his room. He's in a bad mood.

EXTENSION **moody** *adj.*

You are moody today. What's going on?

❼ sharp *adj.*

There was a sharp drop in crime last year.

EXTENSION **Other Usages of *Sharp*:**

I need a sharp knife to cut the beef. (means *can cut things easily*)

I had a sharp pain in my leg a moment ago. (means *short and strong*)

Samantha answered all the questions correctly. She's very sharp. (means *intelligent*)

A. Word Definitions

Use the clues to fill in the blanks with the word choices given. Change the word form if necessary.

philosopher	human	emotion	ability	evidence	according to	fear	mood

1. There is a lot of **evidence** that smoking is bad. (shows something is true)
2. Many scientists study these caves. **Humans** lived here a long time ago. (person)
3. **According to** the weatherman on TV, a storm is coming. (as told by someone)
4. Love is a powerful **emotion**, and it can make people do unusual things. (feeling)
5. The famous English **philosopher** John Locke was born in 1632. (thinker)
6. Many people in Europe have the **ability** to speak several languages. (level of skill)
7. Kathy has a strong **fear** of spiders and snakes. (feeling of being afraid)
8. Terry is always in a bad **mood** on Monday mornings. (state of mind)

B. Words with Different Meanings

Match the word in bold with its definition.

1 The news stories about the car company caused a **sharp** drop in sales. **a**
I need a new knife because my old one isn't **sharp** enough. **b**
Definition: a *adj.* happens suddenly and strongly b *adj.* can cut things easily

2 Doing our homework every night is important. Our teacher puts a lot of **stress** on it. **a**
Students feel a lot of **stress** when they have to take final exams. **b**
Definition: a *n.* special attention to something b *n.* pressure

3 Many pet owners **treat** their animals like their own children. **a**
Jim's father promised to bring him a **treat** from New York. **b**
Definition: a *v.* to act towards someone or something b *n.* something special that you enjoy

C. Multiple Choice

Circle the answers.

1. What did René Descartes think about animals?
   a. Animals could think just like humans.
   b. Animals could learn how to use machines.
   c. Animals had the same feelings as humans.
   (d.) Animals couldn't think like humans.

2. How do animals probably feel when they run away from danger?
   a. They feel angry.
   (b.) They feel afraid.
   c. They feel hungry.
   d. They feel sad.

3. Why did the two penguins at the London Zoo stop eating?
   a. They didn't like the new food.
   b. Their zookeeper suddenly died.
   (c.) Someone took their baby away.
   d. They couldn't feel any emotions.

4. What special thing do rats sometimes do?
   a. Show fear
   b. Sing songs
   (c.) Have fun
   d. Steal things

NOTES

ANSWER KEY Student's Book ▶ p. 64

All in Good Fun

Words & Expressions

Listen and write the sentence number of the activity in the box. Track 35

Free-Time Activities

3

attend a concert

7

watch a sporting event

4

visit a museum

1

go to KTV

9
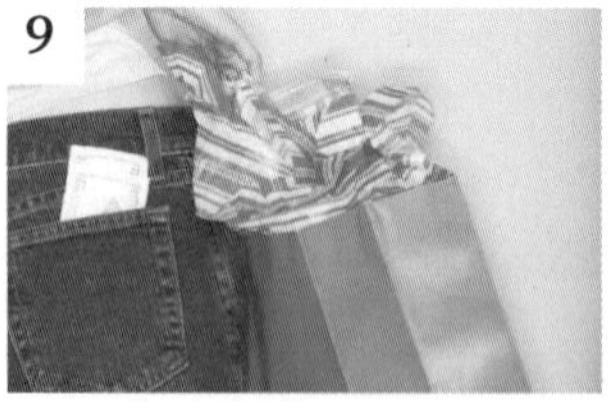
go shopping

12

go to the movies

11

go on a picnic

8

go to a party

2

go to the beach

5

go for a bike ride

6

play a musical instrument

10

play a sport

Practice

Talk to a partner.

- Who joins you at KTV?
- How often do you go for a bike ride?
- What is the best place to go on a picnic?
- Which activities do you like to do with your friends?

Teaching Resources

Audio Transcripts for *Words & Expressions*: Track 35

1. I'm really shy, so I don't like **going to KTV**. I can't sing in front of others.
2. It's summertime! Let's **go to the beach** and enjoy the sun.
3. Every time I **attend** a classical **concert**, I feel very relaxed.
4. **Visiting a museum** is a boring thing to do on vacation.
5. Today is a beautiful day. We should **go for a bike ride** along the river.
6. Susan can't **play** any **musical instruments**. She wants to take piano classes.
7. Jared loves **watching sporting events**. He talks about baseball all the time.
8. I never get a chance to meet new people. Let's **go to a party** tonight!
9. Mike hates **going shopping**. It makes him tired.
10. Do you like exercising? What **sports** do you play?
11. I like to **go on picnics** with my family near the lake.
12. Do you want to **go to the movies**? I want to see the new Robert De Niro film.

More to Teach:

Free-Time Activities: Vocabulary

read	go camping	play computer games
write	go fishing	play cards
cook	go dancing	play (the) guitar
paint	go hiking	play (the) drums
watch TV	go for a walk	visit friends
listen to / play music	go out for a drink	work out
surf the Internet	go out for dinner	rent a video

Free-Time Activities: Sentence Patterns

In my free time, I like (*activity*).	usually with infinitive
I don't really like (*activity*).	gerund / infinitive
I enjoy (*activity*). It's fun.	gerund only
I like (*activity*) with my friends.	gerund / infinitive
My favorite thing to do is (*activity*).	bare infinitive (no **to**)
___________ is my favorite type of music / sport. My favorite type of TV show / movie is ___________.	noun

1. What do you do on weekends?
2. Is your life exciting or boring?
3. How often do you meet up with friends?

Listen Up

Listen and check the information you hear. Track 36

☑ I don't like to ride a bike when the path is too crowded.
☐ My friends and I go on a picnic every two weeks.
☐ I go for a bike ride on weekends.
☐ I enjoy staying home and watching TV.
☑ Sometimes, I relax by reading in the park.

☐ I am a big fan of martial arts.
☑ Checking out art museums is a really interesting activity.
☑ Jazz is my favorite type of music.
☑ I practice playing the guitar in my free time.
☐ I don't like to attend concerts.

Act It Out

Practice the conversations with the word choices given.

attend concerts	watch TV	play a musical instrument		going to the movies
rock	jazz	classical	hip-hop	
the news	sitcoms	movies	sports programs	
piano	guitar	violin	flute	trumpet
action film	drama	comedy	horror film	romance

1. **A:** Do you **attend concerts**?
   B: Yes. I like **rock/jazz/classical/hip-hop** music the most.
2. **A:** How often do you **watch TV**?
   B: I watch TV for an hour every day. I like to watch **the news/sitcoms/movies/sports programs**.
3. **A:** Can you **play a musical instrument**?
   B: Yes. I can play the **piano/guitar/violin/flute/trumpet**. / No, but I want to take **piano/guitar/violin/flute/trumpet** lessons.
4. **A:** Do you enjoy **going to the movies**?
   B: Yes, I do. I usually watch a(n) **action film/drama/comedy/horror film/romance**.

Did You Know...?

Put the words in the appropriate columns. Some words can be used with more than one verb.

a meeting   an amusement park   a friend   a basketball game   a city   a club

go to	attend	visit
a meeting/an amusement park/a basketball game/a city/a club	**a meeting**	**an amusement park/a friend/a city**

Teaching Resources

Audio Transcripts for *Listen Up*: Track 36

Lance

Hi, I'm Lance. I love being outside. I take my bicycle for a ride three times a week. I usually like to ride my bike early in the morning. There are fewer people on the bike path at that time. The ride also helps to wake me up. Every two months, my friends and I go on a picnic together. I sometimes just want to relax, so I read in the park near my house.

Danielle

My name's Danielle, and I'm a big fan of the arts. A day at an art museum would be perfect for me. I like to look at a painting for a long time and try to understand its meaning. I also enjoy attending concerts. I like jazz concerts most of all. When I'm in the mood to stay home, I practice playing the guitar. It's difficult to learn, but I love it.

More to Teach:

Go to is more general than **attend** and **visit**. **Attend** is usually formal. It is used when someone participates in or watches an event. We use **visit** when we go to see a place or person. See more examples below:

go to	attend	visit
a concert	a concert	a museum
a museum	a lecture	a family member
a baseball game	a (formal) party	a client
a party	a funeral	a doctor
a movie theater	a wedding	
a pub	a school	
a funeral		
a wedding		
a school		

Conversation

Making Plans

Listen and fill in the blanks with the word choices given. Track 37

opinion	live	romance	relaxing	delicious	fan

Amanda and Greg are talking about their plans for tonight.

Amanda: Hey, Greg. What are you doing tonight?

Greg: Hi, Amanda. I'm not sure. Would you like to go to a movie?

Amanda: Sure. I love movies. What type of movie?

Greg: Let me think . . . Are you a(n) 1. **fan** of action movies?

Amanda: Action movies aren't my cup of tea. What do you think about seeing a(n) 2. **romance** movie?

Greg: They're not my thing. Maybe seeing a movie isn't a good idea. Do you like going to concerts? There's a concert in the park tonight.

Amanda: That's a great idea. I love listening to 3. **live** music.

Greg: Great. What's your 4. **opinion** of classical music? It's a Bach concert.

Amanda: I like Bach's music a lot. Attending a classical concert sounds very 5. **relaxing**.

Greg: Cool. I can pick you up. Do you want to have dinner before the concert? I know a good Indian restaurant.

Amanda: I'm not a big fan of Indian food. What do you think of having Italian food?

Greg: That sounds good to me. Italian food is 6. **delicious**. See you then.

Amanda: Bye.

Key Words

❶ **fan** *n.*

Cassie is a soccer fan. She watches every Chelsea game.

EXTENSION **Other Usage of *Fan*:**

It's too hot. Turn on the fan. (means *a machine used to cool the air*)

❷ **not one's cup of tea** *phr.* | synonym | not one's thing |

Indian movies are not my cup of tea. I prefer British movies.

❸ **romance** *n.*

Love Actually is Sally's favorite romance movie.

EXTENSION **Other Usage of *Romance*:**

There is a new romance in school. Tara is dating Sam. (means *a love affair*)

romantic *adj.*

We had a romantic dinner in a French restaurant last night.

❹ **concert** *n.*

I went to see a rock concert yesterday. It was great.

❺ **live** *adj., adv.*

The bar has live music on Friday nights.

I like to see my favorite team play live.

EXTENSION **Usage Note:**

Live (*adj.*) and **alive** (*adj.*) both mean "living." **Live** usually refers to animals and normally takes a noun.
He had a terrible accident, but he is **alive**.
There was a **live** chicken in the kitchen.

❻ **opinion** *n.*

Josh always asks his girlfriend for her opinion before he makes a choice.

EXTENSION **in one's opinion** *phr.*

In Dave's opinion, *Pride and Prejudice* is a great novel.

❼ **classical** *adj.*

I studied classical music before I started playing rock.

EXTENSION **Usage Note:**

classical (*adj.*)	traditional
classic (*n.*)	something with a great reputation

Compare the examples below:
I enjoy reading **classical** literature.
This book is a **classic**.

Key Words

8 relaxing *adj.*

Mozart's music is very relaxing. I like to listen to it after work.

EXTENSION **relaxed** *adj.*

Henry is a relaxed person. He never gets angry.

relax *v.*

When you can't sleep, just lie down and try to relax.

relaxation *n.*

The guys went to the countryside for some rest and relaxation.

A. Word Definitions

Use the clues to fill in the blanks with the word choices given.

type	fan	romance	concert	live	opinion	classical	relaxing

1. I didn't like the movie at all. What is your **opinion**? (idea)
2. Listening to **classical** music helps me go to sleep at night. (by Mozart or Bach)
3. Jason is a big **fan** of comic books. He has a collection of them. (really likes)
4. My weekend in the countryside was very **relaxing**. (peaceful)
5. Six different bands are playing in the **concert**. (show)
6. Jenny loves **live** music. She goes to clubs every weekend. (not recorded)
7. I don't like that **type** of food. There is too much oil in it. (kind)
8. This book is a(n) **romance** about a young couple in France. (love)

B. Meanings in Context

Choose the meaning of the sentence in the conversation.

1. I'm not sure.
   - a. There is no doubt.
   - (b.) I don't know.

2. Action movies aren't my cup of tea.
   - (a.) I don't really like them.
   - b. I think they are the best.

3. They are not my thing.
   - a. I lost one of them.
   - (b.) I'm not interested in them.

4. I can pick you up.
   - a. I'm stronger than you are.
   - (b.) I'm able to give you a ride.

5. I'm not a big fan of Indian food.
   - (a.) Indian food isn't my favorite type of food.
   - b. Indian food tastes very good.

6. That sounds good to me.
   - (a.) That's a great idea.
   - b. That's beautiful music.

C. Language Tips

Talking about Likes and Dislikes

Question	Response	
	Likes	***Dislikes***
Do you like . . .? Do you enjoy . . .? Are you a fan of . . .?	I like . . . (very much / a lot). I enjoy . . . I'm a big fan of . . . I'm a big . . . fan. I'm crazy about . . .	I don't like . . . I hate . . . I'm not a fan of . . . . . . is not for me. . . . is not my cup of tea. . . . is not my thing.

Practice the sentence patterns with the choices below.

reading novels	traveling	old movies
collecting stamps	the Internet	Chinese food
talking on the phone	the New York Yankees	knitting

Gerunds and Infinitives

Usage

Both gerunds (Verb + -ing form) and infinitives (to + base form) can be used as the **subject**, **complement**, or **object** of a sentence.

subject	Seeing a movie isn't a good idea. To make mistakes is good for language learning.
complement	James' favorite sport is swimming. Kim's dream is to become a dancer.
object	I love listening to live music. Alex wants to drink some fruit juice.

Usage Note

1. Gerunds are most commonly used as the subject or complement of a sentence.
2. Only gerunds are used as the object of a preposition.

For Example:
What do you think of having Italian food?
~~What do you think of to have Italian food?~~

Signal Words

Verbs are often followed by gerunds or infinitives.

gerunds	admit imagine	avoid keep	consider miss	mind regret	enjoy suggest	finish quit
infinitives	agree hope	ask learn	choose plan	decide promise	expect want	fail need
gerunds or infinitives	continue	begin	start	hate	like	love

Chris **enjoys** fishing with his kid.
Bryan **refused** to go to the meeting.
Mike **hates** shopping / to shop.

Different Meanings

Some verbs can be followed by gerunds or infinitives, but there will be a difference in meaning.

Verb	Example	Meaning
remember	I **remembered** sending the e-mail.	I sent the e-mail, and I remembered the action.
	I **remembered** to send the e-mail.	I needed to send the e-mail, and I did it.
stop	The man **stopped** smoking.	He doesn't smoke anymore.
	The man **stopped** to smoke.	He stopped because he wanted to smoke.
go on	Kate **went on** working as a nurse.	She kept working as a nurse.
	Kate **went on** to work as a nurse.	Her next step was to become a nurse.

A. Fill in the Blanks

Use the gerund or infinitive form of the words given to complete the sentences.

live	speak	take	travel	go	exercise	help	make

1. Dan promised **to take** his son to an amusement park.
2. Felix wants **to travel** all over the world.
3. I avoid **exercising** for more than two hours in the gym.
4. Isaac keeps **making** noise while I'm working.
5. I chose **to live** in the city because it's exciting.
6. How did you learn **to speak** English so well?
7. Tyler always asks **to go** to the bathroom during class.
8. Eva agreed **to help** me with my school project.

B. Complete the Dialogue

Use the words given to complete the dialogue.

enjoy	hope	need	love	miss	suggest	mind	plan

Sandy: I am taking a semester off. I 1. **need** to make money.
Cam: What are you doing?
Sandy: I'm working at the post office. I deliver letters.
Cam: Do you 2. **mind** delivering mails instead of going to school?
Sandy: No. I 3. **enjoy** working at the post office. I also 4. **love** to walk around the neighborhood.
Cam: I 5. **hope** to see you back at school soon, Sandy.
Sandy: Me too. I 6. **miss** seeing my classmates. I 7. **plan** to return next year.
Cam: Well, I 8. **suggest** working hard.
Sandy: Don't worry, Cam. I am a hard worker.

C. Correct the Mistakes

Fix the errors in the passage.

What do you regret the most in your life? A newspaper asked people the question. Many people remembered ~~to quit~~ **quitting** a good job. Some people admitted ~~to leave~~ **leaving** school too early. Others missed ~~to~~ seeing an old boyfriend or girlfriend. Many fathers regret not ~~spend~~ **spending** enough time with their children. They avoided ~~to get~~ **getting** along with them because they were busy. They didn't stop ~~talking~~ **to talk** to their kids. What about you? Start ~~think~~ **thinking/to think** about what is important in your life and decide ~~making~~ **to make** changes.

Teaching Resources

More to Teach:

Infinitive as the Subject

Using an infinitive as the subject of a sentence sounds very formal. It is mostly used in:

1. formal speeches
2. poetic literature

For Example:

To live is to learn.

The Difference

There is a difference in emphasis between **infinitives** and **gerunds**:

1. The **infinitive** form is often used to describe **general ideas** and **goals**.
2. The **gerund** form is mostly used to talk about **reality** and **everyday life**.

This is why there is a separation between the verbs that take each one.

For Example:

Goal / General Idea	I promise **to be** there early. Matt plans **to start** a company next year. Most people refuse **to learn** about computers.

Everyday Life	I like **being** a student. **Playing** basketball is Larry's favorite pastime. Melissa loves **learning** new things.

Usage Note

Two uses often mean the same thing. The only difference is what the sentence emphasizes. Compare the sentences below:

The doctor's job is **to save lives.** (the general idea of the job)
The doctor's job is **saving lives.** (he does it every day)

Reading

Before You Read

Look at the pictures. What are the people doing? What activities do you want to do for exciting?

Make Your Life More Extreme

Track 38

While You Read

1. Which sport takes place in the water?
2. Which sport requires people to run?
3. Which sport do you think is the most dangerous?

Most people agree that ironing is boring. However, would you like to try extreme ironing? Extreme ironing is a little different from normal ironing. Instead of in your home, you do it on a boat, skateboard, or mountain. This is an extreme sport.

An extreme sport is a fun and risky activity. It's also a little dangerous. Take shark cage diving, for example. Divers go into the ocean with great white sharks. The divers stay in a cage. This way, they don't become the shark's lunch.

Everyone knows about the Running of the Bulls. This is an annual event in Pamplona, Spain. Bulls chase participants through the city streets. Injuries are common because the bulls are big, strong, and angry.

Would you like to ride your bike on the Road of Death? This is a road in Bolivia. Locals gave it that name because it is the most dangerous road in the world. It is high up and very narrow. However, some bikers like it because of the adventure and beautiful view.

Do you feel bored with life? Maybe an extreme sport is the answer.

Key Words

❶ **extreme** *adj.*

One of the problems with living in Alaska is the extreme cold.

EXTENSION **extremely** *adv.*

Hilda's mother was extremely nice to me when I was in Germany.

❷ **risky** *adj.*

You shouldn't drive after you drink alcohol. It's too risky.

EXTENSION **risk** *n., v.*

Overweight people have a higher risk of getting heart disease.

I don't want to risk my money on the stock market.

❸ **diving** *n.*

The Philippines has some great places for diving.

EXTENSION **dive** *v.*

Alex dived off the rock into the lake.

diver *n.*

All the divers need to wear an oxygen tank.

❹ **annual** *adj.*

The family trip has become an annual activity. We travel to a different place every year.

❺ **event** *n.*

That music festival is a huge event.

❻ **chase** *v.*

The police chased the thief down the street.

❼ **participant** *n.*

There were eight participants in the discussion.

❽ **injury** *n.*

The basketball player suffered serious leg injuries.

EXTENSION **injure** *v.*

The fire killed five people and injured 27.

injured *adj.*

They took the injured man to the hospital straight away.

❾ **local** *n., adj.*

One of the locals recommended a restaurant to us.

(One of the local people recommended a restaurant to us.)

❿ **adventure** *n.*

We went to Brazil last summer. It was a real adventure.

A. Word Definitions

Use the clues to fill in the blanks with the word choices given. Change the word form if necessary.

agree	extreme	dive	annual	participant	chase	local

1. Bungee jumping is a(n) **extreme** sport in which people jump from a high place. (very unusual and dangerous)
2. I **agree** that knowledge of Chinese is helpful to learn Japanese. (have the same opinion)
3. Some visitors throw trash on the ground. The **locals** are angry about this. (people who live in the place)
4. The man **dived** into the river from a height of 20 meters. (jump into deep water)
5. I always have fun at our **annual** company trip. (yearly)
6. Some scientists **chase** storms to learn about storms. (go after)
7. **Participants** in the survey get gifts from the company. (someone who takes part in an activity)

B. Complete the Passage

Use the correct form of the words given to complete the passage.

risky	injuries	dangerous	adventure

Are you missing something in your life? Do you have extra energy to get rid of? If you said *yes* to these questions, an extreme sport like volcano boarding is perfect for you. Visitors to Nicaragua's Cerro Negro volcano can slide down the mountain at speeds of up to 80 kilometers per hour. Going down an active volcano can be 1. **risky**. Some parts of Cerro Negro are 2. **dangerous**, but the boarding area isn't. 3. **Injuries** can sometimes happen, but it's as safe as snowboarding. Are you ready for a one-of-a-kind 4. **adventure**?

C. Multiple Choice

Circle the answers.

1. Where could extreme ironing be done?
   a. On your balcony
   b. In a convenience store
   (c.) On a skateboard
   d. In your living room

2. What does the article say about shark cage diving?
   a. People oppose shark cage diving.
   (b.) Participants dive with great whites.
   c. It is a boring activity these days.
   d. Divers eat lunch in the cage.

3. What is true about the Running of the Bulls?
   (a.) Injuries happen all the time there.
   b. The bulls run away from participants.
   c. It happens once a month in Pamplona.
   d. The bulls usually stay in a cage.

4. Why do bikers go to the Road of Death?
   a. Their relatives died on the road.
   b. There are bulls on the road.
   (c.) They enjoy the pretty scenery.
   d. It is in a historic valley.

Game Time

Words & Expressions

Listen and write the sentence number of the sport in the box. Track 39

Types of Sports

12

play baseball

1

go golfing

2

play football

6

play volleyball

10

play hockey

7

go bowling

9

go jogging

4

lift weights

11

play badminton

5

do tae kwon do

8

play basketball

3

play soccer

Write the name of the sport in the appropriate columns.

Individual Sport	Team Sport
golf, bowling, jogging, weight lifting, tae kwon do	baseball, football, volleyball, hockey, badminton, basketball, soccer

Practice

Talk to a partner.

- Which of these sports do you play?
- Which sports do you like to watch on TV?
- Which sports do you think are boring?
- Do you think sports are important?

Teaching Resources

Audio Transcripts for *Words & Expressions*: Track 39

1. To play this sport, you have to use a club and a small white ball.
2. This team sport can be dangerous. It's played on a big field.
3. This is the most popular sport in the world. The World Cup is its most important event.
4. You need to have strong arms and legs to pick up the weights.
5. This martial art comes from South Korea. It's popular in Taiwan.
6. Two teams of six players compete in this sport. Many people play it at the beach.
7. In this sport, you roll a ball and try to hit ten pins.
8. Tall people are often good at this sport. Dwight Howard is a good example.
9. Put on a pair of running shoes and go to the park to do this.
10. You'll need ice skates to play this sport.
11. This sport is similar to tennis.
12. In this sport, hit a white ball with a bat. Then start running!

1. What do you do for exercise?
2. Who are your favorite sports stars?
3. Do you like to exercise alone or with friends?

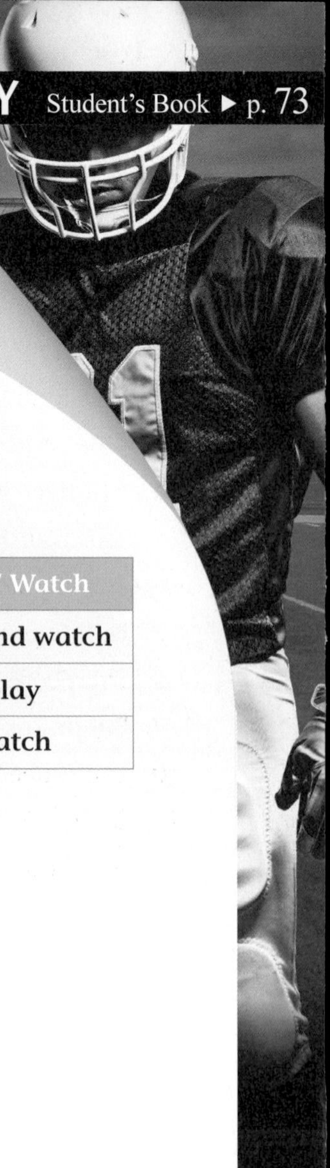

Listen Up

Task I *Listen and complete the chart.* Track 40

Korean	Russian	Brazilian
Moscow	São Paulo	Seoul
golf	hockey	soccer

	Nationality	City	Favorite Sport	Play / Watch
Fabio	**Brazilian**	**São Paulo**	**soccer**	**play and watch**
Shin-soo	**Korean**	**Seoul**	**golf**	**play**
Elena	**Russian**	**Moscow**	**hockey**	**watch**

Task II *Listen again and check **True** or **False**.*

	True	False
1. Fabio is a rich man from Brazil.	☐	☑
2. Golf is the most popular sport in South Korea.	☐	☑
3. Golf is an expensive sport to play in South Korea.	☑	☐
4. Elena is too busy to play a sport.	☑	☐
5. Elena broke her nose twice this year.	☐	☑

Act It Out

Practice the conversations with the word choices given.

football	baseball	basketball	volleyball	hockey
lift weights	do tae kwon do	swim	go mountain climbing	
golfing	bowling	jogging	surfing	
this afternoon	on Saturday	next weekend		

1. A: I often play **football/baseball/basketball/volleyball/hockey** with my friends.
   B: Really? I prefer to **lift weights/do tae kwon do/swim/go mountain climbing**.
2. A: I want to watch a **football/baseball/basketball/volleyball/hockey** game on TV.
   B: You're so lazy. Don't just watch. Go out and play **football/baseball/basketball/volleyball/hockey**.
3. A: I want to go **golfing/bowling/jogging/surfing**, but my friends are busy.
   B: I can go with you. We can do it **this afternoon/on Saturday/next weekend**.

Did You Know...?

Match the sport with the place. Some sports are played in the same place.

a. park	b. field
c. pool	d. gym
e. course	f. court

d 1. lift weights
c 2. go swimming
a 3. go jogging
b 4. play soccer
f 5. play basketball
e 6. go golfing
b 7. play football
f 8. play volleyball

Teaching Resources

Audio Transcripts for *Listen Up*: Track 40

Speaker 1: Fabio

My name is Fabio. I'm 21 years old. I live in **São Paulo**, Brazil. My favorite sport is **soccer**, of course! Soccer is more than a sport in Brazil. It's a way of life. The Brazilian national team is one of the best soccer teams in the world. **I like to watch soccer. I'm a good player too.** It's a cheap sport to play. It's perfect for me because I'm just a student.

Speaker 2: Shin-Soo

I'm Shin-Soo, an 18-year-old college student from **Seoul**. There are many popular sports in South Korea: soccer, baseball, and tae kwon do. My favorite sport is **golf. I don't often watch golf, but I love to play!** It is expensive to play golf in South Korea, so I have to spend all my money on golf. I play pretty well. My coach thinks that I can become a professional golfer.

Speaker 3: Elena

My name is Elena. I'm 20 years old. I go to **Moscow** State University. **I don't have time to play a sport, but I like to watch hockey.** Russia is a cold country. There is a lot of ice in the winter, so people play hockey outside. Hockey is a difficult sport, and it can be dangerous too. My friend Ivan often plays hockey. He broke his nose twice this year! That's why I prefer to watch. It's a lot safer.

More to Teach:

More on Did You Know . . .?

Sport	Place
play tennis	court
play baseball	diamond
play hockey	rink
go bowling	alley
play badminton	court

Conversation

Sports Talk

Listen and fill in the blanks with the word choices given. Track 41

knee	asleep	hard	leading	meet up	a lot

Jerry calls his friend Adam on the phone.

Jerry: Hi, Adam. What's up?

Adam: Hey, Jerry. I was watching a basketball game, but I fell 1. **asleep** . It's almost over.

Jerry: Orlando is playing Miami, right? Who's winning?

Adam: Orlando is 2. **leading** by eight. Miami is pretty weak.

Jerry: Great! I hate Miami. Did you see Saturday's game?

Adam: No. I was busy. I was working out at the gym.

Jerry: You work out 3. **a lot** . Are you still playing basketball?

Adam: A little bit, but my back hurts right now. I hurt it while I was playing basketball with friends on Sunday.

Jerry: That's too bad, man.

Adam: I need to recover and get back in shape.

Jerry: While you were playing basketball, I was watching TV. I have 4. **knee** problems, so I don't exercise enough.

Adam: When I'm healthy, I play a lot. I want to join the school team.

Jerry: Then you should practice 5. **hard** . Basketball requires a lot of skill.

Adam: And you have to be tall.

Jerry: I know. I guess basketball isn't for me. Let's 6. **meet up** and watch a DVD.

Adam: Sounds good.

Key Words

❶ asleep *adj.*

Grandpa was tired after a long day, so he fell asleep on the sofa.

EXTENSION **Usage Note:**

> To **be asleep** is to be sleeping. To **fall asleep** is to go to sleep. **Sleepy** is the feeling of wanting to sleep.
> Quiet! The baby is asleep.
> Walter is sleepy. Let's get him home.

❷ win *v., n.*

We need to win our next game. It's against the Celtics.

The Seattle Mariners had 103 wins last year.

❸ lead *v.*

The Lakers lead the series two games to one.

EXTENSION **Other Usages of *Lead*:**

After we arrived at the restaurant, a waiter led us to our table. (means *take someone somewhere*)

We need a good coach to lead our team. (means *be in charge of*)

❹ work out *phr.* synonym exercise

I usually work out at the gym on Wednesdays.

EXTENSION **Other Usage of *Work Out*:**

Things worked out well. We finally solved the problem. (means *have a good result*)

❺ recover *v.*

Dan is in the hospital. He's still recovering from the operation.

EXTENSION **recovery** *n.*

It took four weeks for my wrist to make a full recovery.

❻ get back in shape *phr.*

I'm really slow. I need to get back in shape.

EXTENSION **Other Phrases with *In Shape*:**

be / keep / stay in shape	She is on a diet to keep in shape.
be out of shape	I'm out of shape. I'm getting fatter.

Key Words

❼ hard *adv.*

Julie works very hard. She is always tired.

EXTENSION **Other Usages of *Hard*:**

Ron kicked the ball hard. (*adv.* with a lot of force)

That math problem was really hard. It took me a long time. (*adj.* difficult)

❽ require *v.*

Growing children require good food and exercise to become strong.

EXTENSION **requirement** *n.*

What are the requirements for the position? I want to apply.

❾ skill *n.*

Language skills are important for certain jobs.

❿ be not for someone *phr.*

Maybe being a swimmer isn't for you. You're not very good in the water.

EXTENSION **Usage Note:**

This phrase is most often used for activities and jobs. It means that the activity or job doesn't suit a person.

A. Words with Different Meanings

Match the word in bold with its definition.

1. The Rangers are **leading** the game. __ⓑ__
   Our tour guide **led** us all over Shanghai. __ⓐ__
   Definition: ⓐ *v.* to take someone somewhere ⓑ *v.* to be winning a game

2. Jamal and his brother play computer games all day. Their muscles are very **weak**. __ⓑ__
   I speak English well, but my writing is **weak**. __ⓐ__
   Definition: ⓐ *adj.* not good ⓑ *adj.* not strong

3. My back **hurts** when I stand up. __ⓐ__
   He **hurt** his knee in the soccer game. __ⓑ__
   Definition: ⓐ *v.* to feel pain ⓑ *v.* to damage something

4. Helen worked **hard** to improve her test scores. __ⓑ__
   This year's exam was very **hard**. Many students failed. __ⓐ__
   Definition: ⓐ *adj.* difficult ⓑ *adv.* with a lot of effort

B. Meanings in Context

Choose the meaning of the sentence in the conversation.

1. It's almost over.
- **a.** It's almost on the top.
- (**b.**) It's close to the end.

2. I was working out at the gym.
- **a.** I had a job at the gym.
- (**b.**) I was exercising at the gym.

3. I need to recover and get back in shape.
- (**a.**) I should get healthy again.
- **b.** I need to cover up my body.

4. Basketball requires a lot of skill.
- (**a.**) Skill is important for basketball.
- **b.** Basketball teaches you many things.

5. I guess basketball isn't for me.
- **a.** This isn't my basketball.
- (**b.**) Basketball is not the right sport for me.

C. Language Tips

Talking about Injuries

Body Part	Incident			Explanation
My (*body part*) hurts.	I	hurt broke injured	my (*body part*).	I have (*body part*) problems. I have a(n) (*body part*) problem. I have (*body part*) pain. I have a bad (*body part*). I have a(n) (*body part*) injury.

Rewrite the sentences using the sentence patterns above. Use different patterns for each blank.

1. My back hurts. ▶ **I have back problems.**
2. Sam broke his ankle. ▶ **Sam has an ankle injury.**
3. I injured my elbow. ▶ **I have a bad elbow.**
4. My mother hurt her knee. ▶ **My mother's knee hurts.**

ANSWER KEY Student's Book ▶ p. 76

Past Continuous Tense

Use the **past continuous tense** to describe longer actions in the past.

Statements

Subject	Past Tense of Be Verb	(Not)	Verb + –ing
I	was	(not)	reading a novel.
You	were	(not)	exercising.
He / She / It	was	(not)	looking at me.
We / You / They	were	(not)	traveling through China.

Questions

Question	Response
Were you studying at university in 2014?	Yes, I was. / No, I wasn't.
Was Nick working last weekend?	Yes, he was. / No, he wasn't.
What were the two boys doing yesterday?	They were studying for a test.
Who was singing in the room?	My younger sister was (singing).

Usage

A short action during a longer action in the past

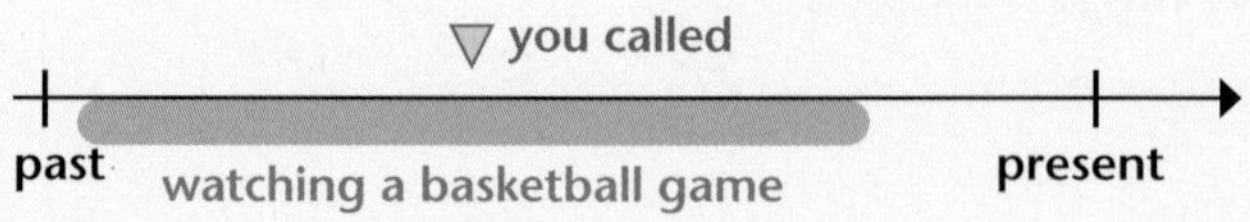

I was watching a basketball game when you called.

A longer action at a certain time

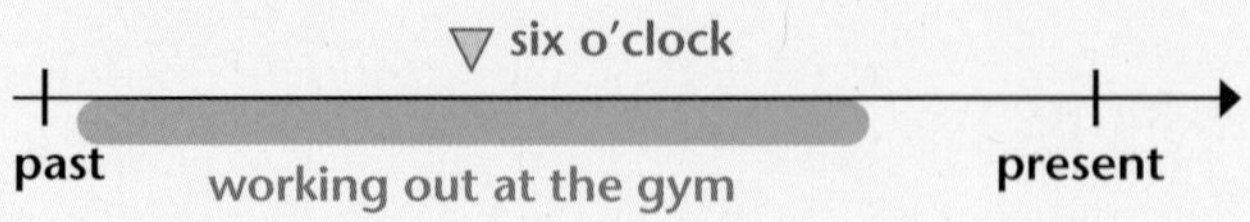

At six o'clock, I was working out at the gym.

Two longer actions at the same time in the past

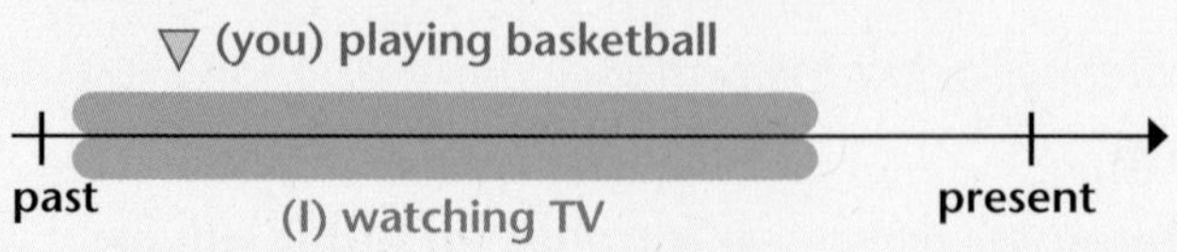

While you were playing basketball, I was watching TV.

A. Match

Match the question with the response.

b	1. Who were you talking to at the park yesterday?	a. He was at the London office.
f	2. Were you playing volleyball on Saturday morning?	b. I was talking to my uncle.
h	3. Why was Alice yelling at Derek this afternoon?	c. Yes. We met at two p.m. in the gym.
c	4. Was the basketball team practicing last Tuesday?	d. I was having lunch with Eva.
d	5. What were you doing at noon on Monday?	e. Alex. He was writing an e-mail.
a	6. Where was Chris working last month?	f. No. I was watching a movie at home.
e	7. Who was using the computer earlier?	g. Yes. They were making fun of his ears.
g	8. Were they making jokes about the boy?	h. He broke her phone.

B. Fill in the Blanks

Change the verb into the past continuous form to complete the sentence.

1. I **was listening** (listen) to music when the phone rang.
2. My parents **were sleeping** (sleep) at the time of the earthquake.
3. Henry **was studying** (study) in the library last Sunday.
4. The man fell asleep while he **was riding** (ride) on the train.
5. At three p.m., I **was singing** (sing) with my friends at KTV.
6. My brothers **were jogging** (jog) yesterday morning.
7. Vicki **was working** (work) all day yesterday.
8. While Ken **was talking** (talk) to Jenny, someone stole his bags.
9. It started to rain while we **were hiking** (hike) in the mountains.

C. Correct the Mistakes

Fix the errors in the story.

I was riding my motorcycle when something bad ~~happening.~~ **happened** A car in front of me stopped quickly. My motorcycle hit the back of the car, and I flew into the air. While I ~~fly~~ **was flying** through the air, I ~~think~~ **thought** about my family. I don't remember much after that. When I woke up, a doctor talked to me. The doctor asked me, "~~Was~~ **Were** you drinking last night?" "I wasn't drinking before I ~~get~~ **got** on my motorcycle," I said. "I ~~read~~ **was reading** at home when my friend invited me to his house." While I was ~~speak,~~ **speaking** the doctor checked my eyes. He told me to be more careful on my motorcycle. While I ~~rode~~ **was riding** home in my wife's car, I ~~feel~~ **felt** thankful for my good luck.

Teaching Resources

More to Teach:

Past Simple vs. Past Continuous

The past simple is the most common way to talk about the past. We only use the past continuous to emphasize continuity.

Tense	Usage	Example
past simple	talk about completed actions in the past	Gina **bought** a car last month. I **didn't talk** to him yesterday.
past continuous	emphasize the continuity of past actions	They **were eating** dinner at five. Ron **was looking** for his keys this morning.

When vs. While

When and **while** have similar meanings, but we usually use the simple past tense after **when** and use the past continuous tense after **while**. See the examples below:

I was sleeping **when** you called. (when + past simple)

While I was sleeping, you called. (while + past continuous)

Other Usages of Past Continuous

The past continuous can mean every moment during a period of time.	I **was studying** all evening yesterday.
It can also mean that an action in the past was temporary.	He **was working** for IBM for a year.
We use it with **always** to talk about things that happened many times.	She **was** always **taking** pictures.

Usage Note

Some verbs are not normally used in the past continuous tense. These verbs are **non-action verbs**. They include **know**, **like**, **need**, **hate**, and **belong**.

For Example:

She really **liked** you.

~~She **was** really **liking** you.~~

Reading

Before You Read

Look at the pictures. Is there anything unusual about the surfer? What do you think the reading is about?

Sports Hero

Track 42

While You Read

1. What happened to Bethany?

2. What is the name of her book?

Do you surf? Bethany Hamilton surfs a lot. Her parents taught her how, and she was in her first competition when she was eight. Even before she was ten, she wanted to be a professional. She entered more competitions and got a company, Rip Curl, to support her.

Then, one day in 2003, a shark attacked her. She lost her left arm and over 60 percent of her blood. She nearly lost her life. Most people are scared of the water after a shark attack. Not Bethany! Just one month later she was back in the water practicing. She kept working towards her goal, kept competing, and turned professional in 2007.

In 2009, she took second place in the Billabong ASP World Junior Championship in Australia. She wrote a book called *Soul Surfer* and was on *The Oprah Winfrey Show*. There is even a movie about her story with Dennis Quaid and Helen Hunt. Bethany is one of the world's top surfers and an inspiration to us all. To find out more about her, go to www.bethanyhamilton.com.

Facts about Bethany Hamilton

Full Name: Bethany Meilani Hamilton
Hometown: Hanalei, Kauai, Hawaii
Born: February eighth, 1990
Height: 187 cm
Weight: 64 kg
Pet: One dog — Hanalei
Motto: "Love life!"

Key Words

❶ **surf** *v.*

Kenting is a perfect place for surfing.

EXTENSION **Other Usage of *Surf*:**

I usually surf the Net to look for information. (means *look through*)

surfer *n.*

The store sells all kinds of clothes for surfers.

---

❷ **competition** *n.*

There is an art competition in the museum.

There is strong competition between those two electronics companies.

EXTENSION **compete** *v.*

Lots of people compete in the 100-meter race. It's very popular.

competitive *adj.*

I don't like playing with Norman. He's so competitive.

---

❸ **professional** *n., adj.* | antonym | amateur |

Paul is a real professional. His work is always good.

I want to be a professional baseball player.

EXTENSION **profession** *n.*

Sulie's dad is a lawyer by profession.

---

❹ **nearly** *adv.* | synonym | almost |

That dog is nearly as big as a person. It's huge!

---

❺ **goal** *n.* | synonym | aim |

The company's goal is to open two new offices this year.

---

❻ **championship** *n.*

Martin Kaymer won the PGA Golf Championship in 2010.

EXTENSION **champion** *n.*

Uruguay was the FIFA World Cup champion in 1930.

---

❼ **inspiration** *n.*

Alice is an inspiration. She is so happy all the time.

EXTENSION **Other Usage of *Inspiration*:**

Where do artists get their inspiration? (means *good ideas*)

inspire *v.*

Music like this can inspire people to learn piano.

inspiring *adj.*

The movie is really inspiring. I see something new every time I watch it.

A. Words with Different Meanings

Match the word in bold with its definition.

1. You can now **surf** the Internet on your cell phone. __b__
   I love to **surf** in Hawaii. The weather there is fantastic! __a__
   Definition: ⓐ *v.* to ride on waves ⓑ *v.* to look through information online

2. As a health **professional**, he works with sick people all day. __a__
   The young skating star became **professional** at age 15. __b__
   Definition: ⓐ *n.* a worker with special training ⓑ *adj.* doing something for pay

3. I'm old enough to **support** myself now. __a__
   I hurt my leg, so I'm wearing an ankle **support**. __b__
   Definition: ⓐ *v.* to give money, food, or housing ⓑ *n.* something to hold a weak part of the body

B. Synonyms

Match the word in bold with its synonym.

competition	contest
nearly	almost
scared	afraid
goal	aim
inspiration	role model

C. Fill in the Blanks

*Use the words in bold from **B** to complete the sentence.*

1. Henry is a great dancer. He won the dancing __**competition**__ last week.
2. Linda doesn't have any pets. She's __**scared**__ of animals.
3. He always helps poor people. He's a(n) __**inspiration**__ to me.
4. The government's __**goal**__ is to give jobs for everybody again.
5. Be careful on the road. I was __**nearly**__ killed last time.

D. Multiple Choice

Circle the answers.

1. When did Bethany start surfing in competitions?
   a. She started when she was 60 years old.
   (b.) Bethany was eight when she started.
   c. Her first competition was in 1990.
   d. Bethany first competed in 2003.

2. What happened when a shark attacked Bethany?
   a. She was killed.
   b. She became less famous.
   c. She started surfing.
   (d.) The shark bit off her left arm.

3. Which statement is NOT true?
   a. Bethany wrote a book.
   b. Her story was made into a movie.
   (c.) She was scared of the water.
   d. She appeared on *The Oprah Winfrey Show*.

4. What is true about Bethany's website?
   (a.) You can learn about Bethany on it.
   b. It shows you how to surf better.
   c. It's the best place to study sharks.
   d. You can help her win championships.

UNIT 10

Rain or Shine

ANSWER KEY Student's Book ▶ p. 80

Words & Expressions

Fill in the blanks with the word choices given.

Nouns	lightning	showers	clouds	Adjectives	foggy	humid	sunny
Verbs	snowing	blowing	raining				

Weather Conditions

2

It's **snowing**.

4

It's **raining**.

5

There are no **clouds**.

8

The wind is **blowing** strongly.

6

It's very hot and **humid** today.

7

There was thunder after the **lightning**.

9

It's really cloudy. There could be **showers**.

3

It's so **foggy**.

1

It's warm and **sunny**.

Listen and write the sentence number in the box. Track 43

Practice

Talk to a partner.

- Do you know any tips on how to prepare for a typhoon?
- Have you seen snowstorm?
- Do you like to go skiing or ice-skating?

Teaching Resources

Audio Transcripts for *Words & Expressions*: Track 43

1. The weather is so nice. It's warm and sunny.
2. Let's go outside and build a snowman.
3. I don't want to drive today. The fog is too thick.
4. Don't forget your umbrella, or you'll get wet.
5. There are no clouds in the sky today.
6. I'm so hot! Let's go to the pool.
7. Don't be scared of the storm. The thunder can't hurt you.
8. It's too windy outside. We should stay home.
9. It may rain a little today, but I don't think you need to wear boots.

More to Teach:

Common Questions and Responses about *Weather*

Question	Response
How's the weather?	It's fantastic!
What's it like out?	It's a little chilly.
What's the weather like?	It is sunny. / The sun is shining.
It's sunny here. What's it like in Chicago?	It's raining.
What's the temperature there?	It's 26 degrees (Celsius).
It's a beautiful day, isn't it?	It sure is.

1. What kind of weather do you like best?
2. How weather affects your mood?
3. Do you watch the weather report on the news?

Listen Up

Task I *Listen and write the places of the city(Prague, Taipei, or Bangkok).* Track 44

Taipei

Bangkok

Prague

Taipei

Prague

Task II *Listen again and fill in the blanks with the word choices given.*

snowy heat wave wet humid storm warm clothes sun foggy

1. Today is a cold and **snowy** day in Prague. It is important to wear **warm clothes**.
2. There is a **storm** in Taipei. It is **wet**. Try to be careful. It's also **foggy** and difficult to see.
3. Bangkok is going through a **heat wave**. It's very hot and **humid**. You shouldn't stay in the **sun** for too long.

Act It Out

Practice the conversations with the word choices given.

spring	summer	fall	winter		
warm	hot	cool	cold		
sky	sun	wind	fog	rain	
clear	sunny	windy	foggy	rainy	
sunglasses	a swimsuit	a scarf	a jacket	a raincoat	an umbrella

1. **A:** My favorite season is **spring/summer/fall/winter**.
   B: Me too. I also like **warm/hot/cool/cold** weather.
2. **A:** Look at the **sky/sun/wind/fog/rain**.
   B: Yeah. It's a **clear/sunny/windy/foggy/rainy** day.
3. **A:** Did you hear the weather report? It's going to be **clear/sunny/windy/foggy/rainy** today.
   B: We need to bring **sunglasses/a swimsuit/a scarf/a jacket/a raincoat/an umbrella**.

Did You Know...?

Noun	Verb	Adjective	Noun	Verb	Adjective
rain	rain	rainy	cloud		cloudy
sun	shine	sunny	fog		foggy
wind	blow	windy	storm		stormy

There is a lot of **snow** today. It's **snowing** today. Today is a **snowy** day.

Teaching Resources

Audio Transcripts for *Listen Up*: Track 44

No. 1

Good morning. This is your Prague weather report for December 31st. Today is a cold day. It will be **snowing** all day. It's windy too. The temperature is minus 15 degrees Celsius. Make sure to wear **warm clothes**. You don't want to get sick.

No. 2

Good morning, listeners. There's a summer **storm** in Taipei today. The weather is **wet**. It's raining heavily, and the wind is blowing. You should also expect thunder and lightning. It's **foggy**, so it's hard to see cars. Be careful when you drive or cross the street.

No. 3

Good morning, Bangkok! Today is one of the hottest days of the year. We're going through a **heat wave**. It's also **humid**. We expect the temperature to reach 35 degrees Celsius. There aren't any clouds in the sky. Don't spend too much time in the **sun**.

More to Teach:

Talking about Weather Conditions

<table>
<tr><td>Good weather</td><td rowspan="6">It's</td><td>sunny / fine / nice / lovely / bright / fair.</td></tr>
<tr><td>There is no rain</td><td>dry.</td></tr>
<tr><td>There is a lot of rain</td><td>wet / rainy.
raining very hard.
raining heavily.
raining cats and dogs.</td></tr>
<tr><td>There are a lot of clouds</td><td>cloudy / gray / dull.</td></tr>
<tr><td>Very hot</td><td>boiling (hot) / extremely hot / scorching.</td></tr>
<tr><td>Cold</td><td>freezing / chilly / frosty.</td></tr>
</table>

A Weekend at the Lake

Listen and fill in the blanks with the word choices given. Track 45

swimsuit	sunny	lightning	fun	check	enough

Sandra and Stacey are talking in the university cafeteria.

Sandra: Hey, Stacey. Do you have plans for the weekend?

Stacey: I want to go to the lake.

Sandra: Sounds like 1. **fun**. Can I join you?

Stacey: Sure. Will you come with John?

Sandra: I'm going to ask him. He looks good in a 2. **swimsuit**.

Stacey: That's cool, but the weather won't be good 3. **enough** to swim on Saturday.

Sandra: Did you 4. **check** the weather report?

Stacey: Of course. It's going to be windy on Saturday. The temperature will be about 20 degrees. It will also be foggy.

Sandra: That's too bad. That's too cold for swimming. How about flying kites?

Stacey: Good idea. The weather will be perfect for that.

Sandra: Really? I hope we don't have 5. **lightning**. It can be dangerous. Is Jason going to come too?

Stacey: Yes, he is. The four of us are going to have a picnic.

Sandra: Wonderful. What are we going to do on Sunday?

Stacey: Sunday will be warm, clear, and 6. **sunny**. That's great weather for swimming.

Sandra: We can go fishing too. Maybe we will have fish for dinner.

Stacey: I can't wait.

Key Words

❶ **fun** *n.*

Ice-skating is a lot of fun. We take the kids to the rink every Saturday.

EXTENSION **Usage Note:**

> **Fun** (*adj.*) is used for something you enjoy doing. **Funny** (*adj.*) is used for things that make you laugh.
> Mountain climbing is fun. I enjoy it.
> The movie was really funny. I laughed the whole time.

❷ **swimsuit** *n.*

I bought a new swimsuit. I want to go to the beach.

❸ **report** *n., v.*

Did you hear the news report? Three people died in a car crash.
If you see an accident, report it to the police.

❹ **windy** *adj.*

It's really windy. My umbrella is broken.

EXTENSION **wind** *n.*
The wind is very strong here in winter.

❺ **temperature** *n.*

Cheese should be kept at low temperatures.

❻ **degree** *n.*

The human body is usually around 37 degrees Celsius.

EXTENSION **Other Usage of *Degree*:**
He has a degree in law, but he works as a photographer. (means a *qualification*)

❼ **foggy** *adj.*

It's so foggy that I can't see my own hands.

EXTENSION **fog** *n.*
Drive carefully. There is a lot of fog on the road.

❽ **sunny** *adj.*

I usually go swimming on sunny days.

❾ **I can't wait (for Noun / to Verb).** *phr.*

I'm really tired. I can't wait to go home.

EXTENSION **Usage Note:**

> **I can't wait for Noun / to Verb** means the same as **I'm looking forward to Noun / Verb + -ing**
> I can't wait for Christmas. (I'm looking forward to Christmas.)
> I can't wait to eat dinner. (I'm looking forward to eating dinner.)

A. Fill in the Blanks

Use the words given to complete the sentences.

warm	lightning	sunny	windy	fog	clear

1. Saturday will be **windy**. The weather will be perfect for flying kites.
2. There will be **fog** on Saturday. It will be difficult to see the sky.
3. Sandra is worried. It is dangerous to fly kites when there is **lightning**.
4. On Sunday, it's going to be **clear**. They will be able to see well.
5. Stacey thinks **sunny** weather is best for swimming.
6. They won't be cold on Sunday. The temperature is going to be **warm**.

B. Word Definitions

Use the clues to fill in the blanks.

1. We're going to the beach this afternoon. Don't forget your **swimsuit**. (wear this in water)
2. The TV station gives weather **reports** every hour. (information)
3. Water starts to boil at a **temperature** of 100 degrees Celsius. (how hot or cold)
4. It's **dangerous** to swim in the lake. The water is too deep. (not safe)
5. We had a **wonderful** time when we went sailing on the bay. (excellent)

C. Meanings in Context

Choose the meaning of the sentence in the conversation.

1. That's cool.
   - (a.) I like it.
   - b. It's not hot.

2. The temperature will be about 20°C.
   - (a.) It'll be warmer or colder than 20°C.
   - b. It'll only be colder than 20°C.

3. Good idea.
   - a. You are kind.
   - (b.) That sounds good.

3. I can't wait.
   - (a.) I'm excited about this.
   - b. I have to go now.

D. Language Tips

Asking about Weather

Did you check the weather report?
How will the weather be?
What will the temperature be next week?
Will it be (*weather adjective*) tomorrow?
What will the weather be like?

Describing Weather Conditions

Good	Bad
The weather will be great.	It'll be windy.
It'll be clear and sunny.	The weather will be cloudy.
It'll be sunny out / outside.	It'll be a rainy day.

Simple Future Tense

Statements

Subject + be + (not) + going to + base form of verb + (*time*).
It's (not) going to be windy on Saturday. Jason is (not) going to come.

Subject + will + (not) + base form of verb + (*time*).
The weather will (not) be good enough to go swimming. David will (not) go to work next Monday.

Usage Note

We often use contractions of **be** and **will** with pronouns in speaking (it's, it'll, we're, we'll, etc.). We also use contractions for **will not** (won't).

Questions

Question	Response
Is Sunday going to be warm? When are they going to arrive?	Yes, it is. / No, it isn't. They're going to arrive at 3:00.
Will you come with John? What will the temperature be on Saturday?	Yes, I will. / No, I won't. It will be about 20 degrees.

Be Going to vs. Will

Usage	Example
be going to or **will** (make predictions)	It's not going to rain tomorrow. It'll be warm and humid. The earth will get warmer in the next ten years.
be going to (talk about plans)	Sylvia is going to meet her friend tomorrow. They're going to build a new house this summer.

Usage Note

We can also use **the present continuous tense** to talk about the future.

For Example:

Mike **is going to visit** his grandparents tomorrow morning.
(Mike **is visiting** his grandparents tomorrow morning.)

Future Time Expressions

today	tomorrow	in January
tonight	tomorrow morning	in two weeks
this summer	next week	on Friday afternoon

A. Match

It's August 20th, and Hans is looking at his calendar. Match the question with the response.

Calendar

	MON	TUE	WED	THUR	FRI	SAT	SUN
8:00							
9:00							

Monday, August 21st

9:00	Meet with Don
11:30	Send a report to Mr. Franks
12:30	Have lunch with Terry at Yuma Bistro
6:30	Meet Rhonda
8:00	Pick up the kids from soccer

Tuesday, August 22nd

6:30	Go to the airport
10:00	Have a meeting
2:45	Get back from Chicago
5:00	Call a customer in Tokyo
7:30	Take the kids to a movie *(you promised)*

__c__ 1. Who is he going to meet for lunch tomorrow?
__a__ 2. Where will he go early Tuesday morning?
__d__ 3. What will he do on Tuesday night?
__b__ 4. When will he send Mr. Franks a report?
__f__ 5. What is he going to do last on Monday?
__e__ 6. Who is he going to call at five o'clock?

a. He's going to go to Chicago.
b. He'll do that on Monday.
c. He's going to eat with Terry.
d. He's going to see a cartoon.
e. He'll phone someone overseas then.
f. He'll go to get his kids at eight o'clock.

B. Correct the Mistakes

Fix the errors in the passage.

The weather for tomorrow [is] going to be cloudy. There will ~~is~~ **be** some rain in the evening. You will ~~to~~ need an umbrella. It's also going [**to**] be cold and windy, so you will ~~having~~ **have** to wear warm clothes. The temperature will [**be**] 13 degrees Celsius. On the weekend, it [**is**] going to be sunny. The weather will be ~~going~~ good for getting out or playing sports. That's great news for most of us. Winter ~~are~~ **is** going to come soon. Enjoy the nice weather. It's not going to ~~lasting~~ **last** much longer.

C. True or False

Listen and check **True** *or* **False**. Track 46

	True	False
1. Matt is going to make an action movie next.	☐	☑
2. Matt is not going to make a movie in the next year.	☑	☐
3. Matt will go back to Australia.	☑	☐
4. Matt is going to relax.	☑	☐
5. Matt will buy a beautiful home in Australia.	☐	☑
6. Matt is going to stay in Australia for several years.	☐	☑
7. Matt is going to make a film about George Washington.	☑	☐
8. Matt will go to work for a radio station.	☐	☑

Teaching Resources

Audio Transcripts for *Grammar Practice*:

C. True or False Track 46

Host: Thanks for coming on our show, Mr. Gibson.

Matt: Sure. By the way, call me Matt.

Host: OK, Matt. People say you're the best actor in Hollywood. What kind of movie are you going to make next? Is it going to be another action film?

Matt: I'm not going to make any movies for a year.

Host: No movies for a year? What are you going to do?

Matt: I'm going to go back to Australia now.

Host: Why?

Matt: I want to get some rest. I have a beautiful home there.

Host: It must be nice. What will you do when you return to America after a year, Mr...., I mean Matt?

Matt: I'm going to make a movie about George Washington.

Host: What a surprise! Anyway, thanks for talking to HGTL Radio. Good luck.

Reading

Before You Read

Look at the pictures. Which place looks the nicest? What do you think the reading is about?

Safe at Home

Track 47

While You Read

1. Why are some houses built differently than others?

2. In what way are Taipei 101's neighbors lucky?

Houses protect people from dangers. They have roofs and walls to keep out bad weather like cold wind or heavy rain. Some houses are built with special protection against natural disasters like typhoons or earthquakes.

Igloos are built by the Inuit people of Canada and Greenland. They are made from snow but are actually quite warm inside because the snow holds air. When the air outside is minus 45 degrees Celsius, the air inside can be a more pleasant 16 degrees Celsius.

Stilt houses offer another kind of protection. These houses are built on long sticks over land or water. They stop flood damage when rivers or lakes rise. They also help to keep rats and other animals out. Stilt houses are still found in Vietnam, Cambodia, and in places in South America.

Taipei 101 is a landmark supertall skyscraper in Taipei, Taiwan. Normally, such a tall building would shake and fall down if typhoons or earthquakes occur. It can withstand natural disasters because it has a tuned mass damper, a huge metal ball. The ball hangs from the 92nd to the 88th floor. When Taipei 101 moves, the ball swings and stops the building from shaking into pieces. Lucky for the neighbors!

Key Words

❶ actually *adv.* synonym | in fact

I thought he was from Australia, but he's actually from New Zealand.

❷ hold *v.*

This bottle holds one liter of water.

EXTENSION **Other Usages of *Hold*:**

The man was holding a can of beer. (means *put in one's hand*)

The annual meeting will be held on November fifth. (means *organize*)

This classroom holds 50 students. (means *have space for*)

I'd like a hot dog, please. Hold the ketchup. (means *not add*)

❸ pleasant *adj.*

Sydney has warm summers and cool winters. You can enjoy a pleasant climate all year round there.

EXTENSION **Other Usage of *Pleasant*:**

Richard is an easy person to work with. He's always pleasant to everyone. (means *friendly*)

❹ stick *n.*

Put down the stick, Theo. You'll hurt your sister.

EXTENSION **Other Usage of *Stick*:**

He stuck posters of his favorite actor all over his bedroom walls. (*v.* attach)

❺ flood *n., v.*

There was a huge flood here ten years ago.

The cities were flooded during the typhoon.

❻ damage *n., v.*

The car accident caused serious damage to his brain. He has problems talking now.

Fatty foods can damage your health.

❼ rise *v., n.*

Some small islands are disappearing as the sea levels continue to rise every year.

We were lucky to see the rise of a full moon.

❽ swing *v.*

Look at the monkey. It's swinging from the tree.

EXTENSION **Other Usage of *Swing*:**

My little sister likes to play on the swings in the park. (*n.* a kind of park equipment that children sit on to go up and down)

A. Fill in the Blanks

Use the words given to complete the sentences. Change the word form if necessary.

stick	flood	damage	rise

1. Sales **rise** every year around Christmas.
2. The driver is fine, but there is a lot of **damage** to the car.
3. After two days of heavy rain, the town was **flooded**.
4. You can make a fire by rubbing **sticks** together, but it takes a long time.
5. The **flood** killed a lot of people in the village.
6. Don't **stick** your finger in your nose! It's very rude.
7. There was a **rise** in food prices last year.
8. Listening to loud music can **damage** your ears.

B. Word Definitions

Use the clues to fill in the blanks with the word choices given.

actually	minus	pleasant	protective	earthquake	metal	hang	swing

1. A(n) **earthquake** in China in the 1500s killed nearly one million people. (shaking of the earth)
2. A lot of children would like to **swing** from tree to tree like a monkey. (move from one side to another)
3. Ray looks pretty young, but he's **actually** 40 years old. (in fact)
4. Don't go outside! It's **minus** 20 degrees out there. (below zero)
5. Some people keep their phones in **protective** cases because they don't want them to break. (safe)
6. The roof is made of **metal**. It's really loud when it rains. (a hard, shiny material)
7. The Striebers have a very **pleasant** house in the woods. I went there with them last winter. (comfortable)
8. Beautiful pictures **hang** in the hall. (be suspended)

C. Classification

Write the type of house next to the matching statement.

ⓐ igloos

ⓑ stilt houses

ⓒ tall buildings

1. These houses which are built over the ground keep people safe from rats and other animals. **ⓑ**
2. Special homes like these have a roof made from ice. **ⓐ**
3. These houses have special protection for not shaking against typhoons or earthquakes. **ⓒ**
4. You can see these houses in Cambodia. **ⓑ**
5. The walls of these houses are cold, but they still have warm air inside. **ⓐ**
6. These can have more than 100 floors. **ⓒ**
7. If you live in a very cold place, this is a good house for you. **ⓐ**
8. These houses are built on sticks over water or land. **ⓑ**

NOTES

UNIT 11 Eating Out

Words & Expressions

Menu Sections

Task I *Listen and write the sentence number in the box.* Track 48

Harris Ranch Diner

3	Starters	French fries, potato skins, Buffalo wings
4	Soups	vegetable, French onion, soup of the day
1	Salads	Caesar, garden, broccoli
5	Main dishes	burger, spaghetti, steak, turkey
6	Desserts	chocolate cake, tiramisu, ice cream
2	Drinks	soda, fresh fruit juice, beer

Business hours: 11 a.m. to 11:30 p.m. every day
313 Pacific Lane, Stockton, CO 72843
(652) 717-3005

Task II *Complete the sentences with the menu sections from above. Change the word form if necessary.*

1. We eat a **starter** at the beginning of a meal.
2. **Desserts** are usually sweet. The waiter serves them after a meal.
3. You can find different vegetables in **salads**.
4. Green tea is one of Darren's favorite **drinks**.
5. **Main dishes** are the biggest part of a meal. They'll fill your stomach.
6. We use a spoon, not a fork, to have **soup**.

Practice

Talk to a partner.

- What would you order from the menu?
- Which menu options are healthy? Which are not?
- How late does the restaurant stay open on Thursdays?

Teaching Resources

Audio Transcripts for *Words & Expressions*: Track 48

1. Neil is trying to lose weight, so he usually has **salad**.
2. Would you like anything to **drink**? We have soda, fruit juice, and five different kinds of beer.
3. We offer a free **starter** with the purchase of any two steaks.
4. It is a cold day, so Chris really wants a hot bowl of **soup**.
5. Turkey is the **main dish** in a Thanksgiving meal.
6. I'm full. I don't have enough room for **dessert**.

More to Teach:

Restaurant Vocabulary

starter	=	appetizer	Cheese sticks are the most popular **starter** in our restaurant.
drink	=	beverage	They sell all kinds of soft **drinks**, like soda and lemonade.
main dish	=	main course entrée	I'll have the smoked salmon for my **main dish**.
side	=	side order	We'd like a **side order** of onion rings.

special	a dish which is not on the regular menu; usually different every day	Today's lunch **special** is roast chicken.
specialty	a dish that a restaurant or place is famous for; on the regular menu	You should try the beef noodle soup. It is this restaurant's **specialty**.

Usage Note

Food is mostly used as a *non-count* noun, even for different types of food in one place.

There is a lot of **food** on the table. (eggs, bread, fruit, etc.)

We use **foods** (count) when we compare types of food or food from different countries, or pick one food from a group.

The **foods** of Spain and Mexico are very different.

Cheese is one of my favorite **foods**.

1. What's the best restaurant in your hometown?
2. How many times do you eat out each week?
3. Where would you take someone on a first date?

Listen Up

Task I *Listen and write the dialogue number and the menu section.* Track 49

1 **desserts**

5 **salads**

2 **soups**

3 **starters**

4 **drinks**

6 **main dishes**

Task II *Listen and check* ***True*** *or* ***False****.*

	True	False
1. Amelia didn't eat anything today.	☐	☑
2. Natalie is ordering small size.	☐	☑
3. Phil and Pete need more time to decide on their main dishes.	☑	☐
4. Chris has something to drink.	☐	☑
5. The man orders blue cheese dressing.	☐	☑
6. Deborah and Tony both want to eat a lot of food.	☑	☐

Act It Out

Practice the conversations with the word choices given.

starter soup salad main dish
some French fries the soup of the day
the Greek salad the pasta
steak house café buffet sushi bar
steaks sandwiches lobster sashimi
juice soda coffee beer wine

1. **A:** Do you want a starter/soup/salad/main dish?
   B: Sure. I would like some French fries/the soup of the day/the Greek salad/the pasta, please.
2. **A:** I know a good steak house/café/buffet/sushi bar on 19th Avenue.
   B: Oh yeah. That restaurant's steaks/sandwiches/lobster/sashimi is / are great.
3. **A:** Would you like something to drink?
   B: Yes. What types of juice/soda/coffee/beer/wine do you have?

Did You Know...?

Would you like, could you, *and* ***could / may I*** *are more polite than* ***do you want, can you,*** *and* ***can I.***

Practice saying the following sentences in a more polite way.

1. Can I take your coat? **(Could / May)**
2. Do you want fries with your meal? **(Would you like)**
3. Can you hold on for a second? **(Could)**
4. I want two bowls of soup. **(I would like)**

Teaching Resources

Audio Transcripts for *Listen Up*: Track 49

Dialogue 1:

Amelia: I ate a lot today. I don't want to eat ice cream.

Bob: But look, Amelia — they have your favorite, cookies and cream! And it's such a hot day.

Amelia: Maybe we can order one to share then. What do you think?

Bob: Let's do it.

Dialogue 2:

Luke: Do you want a big bowl or a small one, Natalie?

Natalie: I want a big one. I need something to really warm my stomach.

Luke: Yeah, me too. I can't wait. I hope it doesn't burn my tongue though.

Dialogue 3:

Pete: What do you want to eat, Phil?

Phil: I'm not sure. Why don't we order something small first, Pete?

Pete: Good idea. That would give us more time to decide on our main dishes. How do the Buffalo wings sound?

Phil: They sound good to me.

Dialogue 4:

Chris: I just went to the gym, and the water machine there was broken.

Mike: Wow! You must be thirsty, Chris.

Chris: Yep. I'm going to get a large glass of juice.

Mike: I want some juice too. I'll call the waiter over.

Dialogue 5:

David: What type of dressing do you have?

Waiter: We have Caesar, Italian, Thousand Island, and blue cheese.

David: I'll have Caesar.

Waiter: Sure. I'll be back in a moment.

Dialogue 6:

Deborah: I'm so hungry. Are you, Tony?

Tony: Yes, Deborah. I didn't have lunch today. What do you want to get?

Deborah: I want a big plate of spaghetti. You?

Tony: I'm going to get the cheese pizza.

Conversation

Dinner Date

Listen and fill in the blanks with the word choices given. Track 50

order	recommend	fine	drink	popular	waitress

Jimmy and Daphne are in a restaurant.

Jimmy: Something smells delicious in here.

Daphne: You're right. I can't wait to order. Oh, our waitress is coming.

Nicole: Hello. Welcome to Barney's Burgers. I'm Nicole, your 1. **waitress** for the evening. May I get you something to start?

Daphne: We'll start with the French fries. It's our first time at this restaurant. Could you 2. **recommend** any main dishes?

Nicole: Everything is good here, but I really like the chicken sandwich. Or you could try our bacon cheeseburger and mushroom burger. Both are very 3. **popular**.

Daphne: OK. I would like the bacon cheeseburger. Hold the tomatoes, please.

Nicole: Sure. One bacon cheeseburger. Hold the tomatoes. How about you, sir?

Jimmy: I'll have the chicken sandwich. Could you give me extra barbecue sauce on the side?

Nicole: Of course. I can add some to your 4. **order**.

Jimmy: Sounds good. Thank you.

Nicole: Do you want anything to 5. **drink**?

Jimmy: No, thank you. Water is 6. **fine**.

Daphne: I'll have a cup of coffee. Can I have it right away?

Nicole: No problem. Your order should be here in about ten minutes.

Key Words

❶ delicious *adj.* | synonyms | tasty, yummy |

The meal looks delicious. My mouth is watering.

❷ order *v., n.*

Anne ordered a medium Coke.

Did the waiter take your order?

EXTENSION **Other Usages of *Order*:**

The doctor ordered Nancy to rest for a few days. (means *tell someone that they must do something*)

You should do things in order of importance. (means *sequence*)

Samuel practiced basketball every day in order to become a professional player. (used to show purpose)

❸ dish *n.*

The menu includes all kinds of tofu dishes.

EXTENSION **Other Usage of *Dish*:**

My brother and I take turns washing the dishes. (means *all the dirty plates, cups, bowls, etc.*)

❹ extra *adj., pron., adv.*

I always allow extra time for my trip. I don't like to rush when traveling.

You don't need to pay extra. The wine is included in the meal.

Hank was really hungry. He ordered an extra large pizza.

❺ sauce *n.*

The chicken tastes good with the Japanese sauce.

❻ add *v.*

The soup is too salty. You need to add some water.

❼ fine *adj.*

Your car is fine. You don't need to buy a new one.

EXTENSION **Other Usages of *Fine*:**

This is a fine house. It's beautiful. (means *very good*)

It's fine out today. Let's go for a run. (means *sunny, not raining*)

Usage Note:

Fine can also be used as an *adverb*. It means "OK" or "well."
Jack broke his leg a few months ago, but he can walk fine now.
I'd like something quick to eat. A sandwich will do fine.

❽ right away *phr.* | synonyms | right now, immediately, at once |

Richard is looking for you. You should call him right away.

A. Word Definitions

Use the clues to fill in the blanks with the word choices given.

order	waitress	recommend	dish	bacon	popular	extra	add

1. Can you **recommend** a movie for children? (suggest)
2. I'd like some **extra** sauce with my steak, please. (more)
3. What are you going to **order** for dessert? (ask for)
4. My meal tastes good, but the cook should **add** some salt next time. (put in)
5. The fried chicken is the cheapest **dish** on the menu. (food)
6. The garden salad is very **popular** with young women. (many people like it)
7. When you see the **waitress**, please ask her for more coffee. (restaurant worker)
8. The **bacon** on that cheeseburger isn't good for you. (type of meat)

B. Meanings in Context

Choose the meaning of the sentence in the conversation.

1. I can't wait to order.
   a. The service is so slow. Let's leave.
   (b.) I'm really hungry.

2. It's our first time at this restaurant.
   (a.) We haven't eaten here before.
   b. We got here very early.

3. Hold the tomatoes, please.
   a. I'd like some extra tomatoes.
   (b.) Don't put any tomatoes on it.

4. Could you give me extra barbecue sauce on the side?
   (a.) Could I have more sauce in a small dish?
   b. Could you put less sauce on my food?

C. Language Tips

Ordering a Meal

A Waiter Might Say . . .	A Customer Might Say . . .
May I get you something to start? Are you ready to order? Our soup of the day is (kind of soup). And for your main course / drink / dessert? Do you want anything to drink? Your order should be here in a few minutes.	I'll start with / I'd like to start with (kind of starters). I would like / I'll have / I'd like to have (kind of main dishes). Does it / that come with (kind of side dishes)? What kinds of (kind of drinks) are there?

Indefinite Pronouns

Words like **something, anybody, both,** and **any** are indefinite pronouns. We use them in place of nouns. Some indefinite pronouns can be singular or plural. When they replace a singular (plural) noun, use a singular (plural) verb.

Singular Indefinite Pronouns (use a singular verb)

something	everything	anything	nothing	someone
one	everyone/everybody	anyone/anybody	no one/nobody	another

Something smells delicious in here.
Everything is good here.
Do you want anything to drink?
Nobody knows the manager's age.
I already had a cup of coffee this morning, but I want to have another.

Plural Indefinite Pronouns (use a plural verb)

both	few	many	others	several

You should try our bacon cheeseburger and mushroom burger. Both are very popular.
A few students take the subway, but many take the bus.
The cameras are expensive. Several cost over $1,000.

Singular or Plural Indefinite Pronouns (use a singular or a plural verb)

some	any	all

Would you like to have tea? There is some in the kitchen. (singular)
The director made a lot of action movies. Some were really successful. (plural)
Could you bring a cup from the kitchen? Any is fine. (singular)
Look at those great jackets! Are any on sale? (plural)

Usage Note

Indefinite pronouns usually take the place of nouns. Some, however, can do other things in a sentence.

I have many classmates, and **some** are my best friends. (indefinite pronoun)
Some animals at the zoo are dangerous. (determiner)

Ted has two sisters, and **both** are very pretty. (indefinite pronoun)
Both apartments have a large bathroom. (determiner)

A. Fill in the Blanks

Use the words ***something, anything, nothing, somebody, anybody,*** *or* ***nobody*** *to complete the sentences.*

1. There's a message on the phone. Maybe **somebody** wants to buy your car.
2. The machine is broken. **Nothing** happens when I push the button.
3. I don't know **anybody** from Australia.
4. Beverly looks worried. **Something** is bothering her.
5. I went to the shopping mall, but I didn't really need **anything**.
6. The bookstore was open, but **nobody** was inside.

B. Match

Match the question / statement with the response.

h 1. Not many students got good marks.
e 2. How many people like pizza?
f 3. Which one do you like?
g 4. Several are very cheap.
b 5. What is on sale in the store?
c 6. How many bikes in the shop have lights?
a 7. Is one of your friends a doctor?
d 8. There are lots of movies to see.

a. Yes. Another is a computer engineer.
b. Everything is ten percent off.
c. Some have them.
d. Are any funny?
e. I think everyone does.
f. Both are beautiful.
g. Yeah. They cost less than $20.
h. That's right. Few passed the test.

C. Correct the Mistakes

Fix the errors in the article.

Cats and dogs are popular pets. Both ~~is~~ **are** good pets, but many people like just ~~another~~ **one**. Some ~~likes~~ **like** dogs and ~~other~~ **others** are cat lovers. Few ~~is~~ **are** fans of both.

There are many different kinds of dogs. Some ~~weighs~~ **weigh** more than 100 pounds, while other types of dogs are small. Their hair is different too. A golden retriever's hair is long. A bulldog has short hair. ~~Anyone~~ **Everyone** loves puppies. Everything about puppies ~~are~~ **is** cute. But few ~~stays~~ **stay** cute. They become big dogs.

Cats aren't as different as dogs. Many ~~is~~ **are** the same size. However, they can be different colors. Look at the cats in a pet store. One is white. Another ~~are~~ **is** black. And some ~~is~~ **are** many different colors. Of course, ~~somebody~~ **everybody** thinks kittens are cute.

Teaching Resources

More to Teach:

Anybody vs. Somebody

Here are some more examples with explanations:

Does **anybody** help him with his work? (general question)

Does **somebody** help him with his work? (he can't do it alone)

Anybody can drive this car. (it's easy to drive)

Somebody drives this car. (one particular person)

Anything vs. Something

Here are some more examples with explanations:

Is there **anything** we can do? (I don't know what)

That's **something** we can do tomorrow. (definite thing)

Reading

Before You Read

Look at the pictures. Have you tried one of these food? Have you had any difficulties eating foods in foreign countries?

Going to Restaurants around the World

Track 51

While You Read

1. How do you pay the bill in France? How about Thailand?

2. If you don't want to have any more drinks in Japan, what should you do?

Food is an important part of a culture, and one of the best ways to enjoy it is in a local restaurant. Every culture has its own table manners. Remember that in different countries, people eat differently.

In India, most people eat with their hands. Wash your hands first! You must use the right hand to eat because Indians think that the left is not clean. Do not touch other people's food or offer them yours. Eating beef and pork is prohibited — a lot of people in India are Hindu or Muslim.

Thai food is for sharing. Don't ask for your own dish. Take enough for a bite or two and eat slowly. The oldest woman should order, and the richest person pays.

Don't pour your own drink in Japan. Your companions will pour it for you. If you don't want any more, leave your glass full. When you pay the bill in Japan, you shouldn't count your change.

French cooks don't like it when you ask for ketchup. You should try the meal first. During your meal, your hands should be visible at all times. Most French people split the bill. You should pay an equal amount, not ask everyone what they ate.

Key Words

❶ **bite** *n., v.*

I didn't have time for lunch. I just took a bite of a sandwich.

A mosquito bit me while I was taking a nap on the park bench.

❷ **pour** *v.*

The milk went bad, so I poured it out.

EXTENSION **Other Usages of *Pour*:**

The house was on fire. Smoke was pouring out of the door. (means *come out*)

It's pouring now. We should stay inside. (means *rain heavily*)

❸ **companion** *n.*

Jason's cat is his closest companion. They spend a lot of time together.

❹ **bill** *n.*

I usually pay my phone bills at the convenience store.

EXTENSION **Other Usages of *Bill*:**

This bill will bring in more tax money. (means *a proposal for a new law*)

I don't have coins. Can you change a ten-dollar bill? (means *paper money*)

❺ **count** *v.*

I counted five different types of birds on the island.

EXTENSION **Other Usages of *Count*:**

Jeff is a great guy. I count him as one of my best friends. (means *consider*)

Tell me what you think. Your opinion really counts. (means *be important*)

❻ **visible** *adj.*

Mars is visible for 24 out of every 26 months.

❼ **at all times** *phr.* synonym always

Keep your head and arms inside the train at all times.

❽ **split** *v.*

The teacher split the students into three groups.

EXTENSION **Other Usage of *Split*:**

The couple split up last month. They didn't love each other anymore. (means *break up*)

❾ **equal** *adj.*

The two stones are equal in size.

EXTENSION **Other Usage of *Equal*:**

All men are equal. (means *having the same rights*)

A. Words with Different Meanings

Match the word in bold with its definition.

1. Her story was reported in the **local** newspaper. __ⓐ__
   One of the best parts of visiting a country is talking with the **locals**. __ⓑ__
   Definition: ⓐ *adj.* related to a particular area ⓑ *n.* a person who lives in a particular area

2. Valerie took a big **bite** of French bread. __ⓑ__
   The man saw a doctor after the dog **bit** him. __ⓐ__
   Definition: ⓐ *v.* to cut something with your teeth ⓑ *n.* the act of using your teeth to cut something

3. We were both full after such a big dinner, so we asked for the **bill**. __ⓑ__
   This isn't a real 100-dollar **bill**, so the bank won't take it. __ⓐ__
   Definition: ⓐ *n.* paper money ⓑ *n.* a list of charges

4. Men and women should have **equal** rights. __ⓐ__
   The baskets have an **equal** number of Easter eggs in them. __ⓑ__
   Definition: ⓐ *adj.* being treated the same ⓑ *adj.* of the same size, amount, or value

B. Word Definitions

Use the clues to fill in the blanks with the word choices given. Change the word form if necessary.

offer	appropriate	pour	companion	visible	at all times	split

1. The woman might be in danger, so the police are staying outside of her house **at all times**. (always)
2. We should **split** the cake into eight pieces. Everyone should get one slice. (divide)
3. It's not **appropriate** to wear shorts. This is a formal dinner party. (suitable)
4. Dogs are great **companions**. You should get one. (friend)
5. That advertisement is **visible** from the other side of the highway. (easy to see)
6. The host **offered** Bob something to drink. (provide)
7. The waitress **poured** drinks for the customers. (fill a cup with a drink)

C. True or False

*Check **True** or **False**.*

	True	False
1. Never touch another person's dish at the table in India.	☑	☐
2. You shouldn't order a steak or some bacon in India.	☑	☐
3. The right hand is considered to be unclean in India.	☐	☑
4. In Thai culture, all dishes are shared.	☑	☐
5. In Japan, do not fill your own glass.	☑	☐
6. French chefs will be happy to offer ketchup to customers.	☐	☑
7. You shouldn't put your hands under the table in France.	☑	☐
8. French people like to share the bill.	☑	☐

NOTES

UNIT 12

School Life

ANSWER KEY Student's Book ▶ p. 96

Words & Expressions

Listen and write the personality words you hear in the blanks. Track 52

friendly	gentle	independent	risk taker	hardworking	generous
serious	negative	fun-loving	patient	talented	careful

Personality Traits

1. 
gentle

2. 
risk taker

3. 
patient

4. 
independent

5. 
hardworking

6. 
generous

7. 
fun-loving

8. 
talented

9. 
friendly

10. 
careful

11. 
negative

12. 
serious

Practice

Talk to a partner.

- Which personality types are good?
- What do your friends say about you? Which adjectives do they use?

Teaching Resources

Audio Transcripts for *Words & Expressions*: Track 52

1. My elder sister is a great nurse. She is **gentle** with her patients.
2. Dave is a **risk taker**. He always does crazy things.
3. Martha is an elementary school teacher. She is **patient** with all the students.
4. Mandy is **independent**. She works part-time at a restaurant. She pays for college without her parents' help.
5. I am a **hardworking** person. I like to be busy all the time.
6. You're paying for lunch? Thank you, my friend. You are too **generous**.
7. Jill often goes to parties. She is such a **fun-loving** girl.
8. You should be a musician. You are so **talented**!
9. Marty has a lot of friends. It's not surprising. He's really **friendly**!
10. Jane thinks hard before she decides anything. She's a **careful** person.
11. My boyfriend Dan is so **negative**. He loves to complain.
12. Daniel is too **serious**. He doesn't know how to have fun.

More to Teach:

Word	Antonym	Word	Antonym
gentle	violent / rough	talented	untalented
risk taker	careful person	friendly	mean
patient	impatient	careful	careless
independent	dependent	negative	positive
hardworking	lazy	serious	fun-loving
generous	cheap	confident	shy
fun-loving	serious	funny	boring

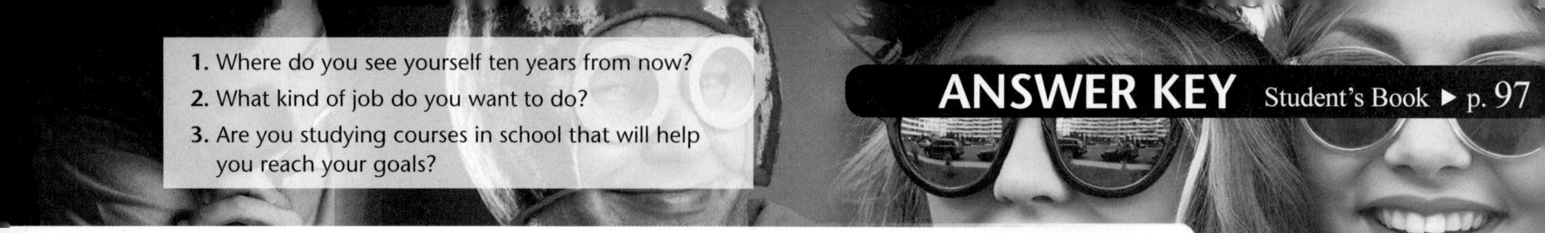

1. Where do you see yourself ten years from now?
2. What kind of job do you want to do?
3. Are you studying courses in school that will help you reach your goals?

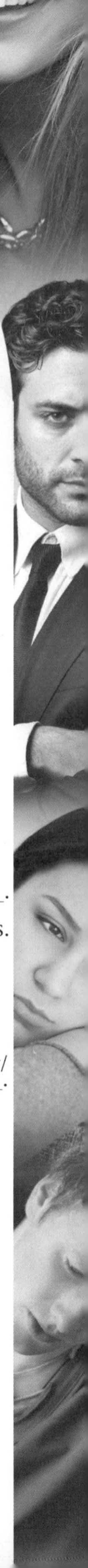

Listen Up

Task I *Listen and complete the sentences with the words you hear.* Track 53

Dialogue 1	1. John wants to change his **major** to business. 2. Sara advises John to study **math**.
Dialogue 2	3. Gordon needs to buy flowers for his **girlfriend**. 4. Marc **lent** $100 to Gordon several days ago.
Dialogue 3	5. Claire plays the **violin**. 6. It is sometimes difficult to find work as a(n) **musician**.

Task II *Listen again and write the name next to the matching personality description.*

John **Marc** **Gordon** **Claire**

1. **John** is not confident.
2. **John** is a careful person.
3. **Marc** thinks Gordon is generous.
4. **Gordon** borrowed money from Marc.
5. **Claire** is a hardworking person.
6. **Gordon** likes to buy things for people.

Act It Out

Practice the conversations with the word choices given.

generous confident fun-loving risk-taking

likes to share believes in himself (herself)
loves to go to parties tries new things often

cheap negative serious careful

doesn't like to spend money is never happy
doesn't smile often seldom takes risks

1. **A:** Is (*name*) a **generous/confident/fun-loving/risk-taking** person?
   B: Yes. He / She **likes to share/believes in himself (herself)/loves to go to parties/tries new things often**.
2. **A:** You are too **cheap/negative/serious/careful** sometimes.
   B: Maybe you're right. I'm not **generous/confident/fun-loving/risk-taking** (antonym) enough.
3. **A:** (*Name*) is quite **cheap/negative/serious/careful**.
   B: Yeah, he / she **doesn't like to spend money/is never happy/doesn't smile often/seldom takes risks**.

Did You Know...?

Fill in the blanks with the word choices given.

fun-loving	risk taker	talented	hardworking	make friends	risk-taking

1. He is a **risk taker**. He takes risks. He is a **risk-taking** person.
2. She is **talented**. She has a talent.
3. I work hard. I am a **hardworking** person.
4. We love fun. We're a group of **fun-loving** people.
5. They are friendly. They **make friends** easily.

Teaching Resources

Audio Transcripts for *Listen Up*: Track 53

Dialogue 1:

John: Sara, you know me well. Should I change my **major** from math to business? I can't decide.

Sara: Tell me, John, are you a risk taker?

John: Not really. I'm usually pretty careful.

Sara: Businessmen have to take risks sometimes. Are you a confident person?

John: Of course not! I'm never sure of anything.

Sara: **Math** would be perfect for you, my friend.

Dialogue 2:

Marc: Hey, Gordon. Where are you going?

Gordon: I'm going to the store, Marc. I need to buy flowers for my **girlfriend**.

Marc: That's cool. You're a generous person.

Gordon: Everybody should give a girl flowers sometimes.

Marc: I never do.

Gordon: That's because you're cheap.

Marc: Maybe. But I **lent** you $100 last week, remember?

Gordon: Dude, I'm joking. Don't be serious.

Dialogue 3:

Claire: Hey, Bill. I need to go to my **violin** practice.

Bill: You're always so busy, Claire.

Claire: I know. I feel so tired. It's hard for **musicians** to find a job. I should just give up.

Bill: Don't be so negative. You're talented and very hardworking. You're going to be a famous musician. I just know it.

Claire: Thanks, Bill. Look. I really have to run.

More to Teach:

Usages of *Like*

What's she like?	This is used generally. It asks for a character description. (friendly, shy, gentle, independent)
What does she look like?	This asks for a physical description. (tall, blonde, thin, attractive)
What does she like?	This asks about the person's interests or hobbies. (soccer, music, cooking, go surfing)

Conversation

Tell Me What to Do

Listen and fill in the blanks with the word choices given. Track 54

goal	hardworking	confident	drop	experience	trouble

A student comes into an advisor's office.

Advisor: Hi, Rachel. How can I help you?

Rachel: Hello. I'm having 1. **trouble** with my schoolwork. The midterms are coming up.

Advisor: You're a 2. **hardworking** student. You'll do great.

Rachel: I'm taking too many classes this semester. I also have a part-time job at a bank. I aim to get some real-world 3. **experience**, but I'm under a lot of stress. I'm having difficulty finding enough time to do everything.

Advisor: Can you leave your job?

Rachel: I need the money.

Advisor: If you take out student loans, you don't need to work.

Rachel: My 4. **goal** is to find a good job in finance. If I keep my job, I might make it happen.

Advisor: You should just 5. **drop** one class.

Rachel: But which class? The deadline is around the corner. I might fail all my classes!

Advisor: Don't be so negative. You should feel more 6. **confident** about yourself. Why don't you take two weeks off? If your boss likes you, he will let you.

Rachel: That's a good idea. Thanks for the advice!

Key Words

❶ **have trouble** *phr.*

I'm having trouble sleeping. I'm so tired.

EXTENSION **get into trouble** *phr.*

The naughty boy often gets into trouble at school.

be in (big / serious) trouble *phr.*

The next time you're late, you're going to be in serious trouble.

❷ **midterm** *n.*

We just finished our midterms. I think I passed.

❸ **be coming up** *phr.* | synonym | be around the corner |

Mother's Day is coming up. I need to buy a gift.

❹ **hardworking** *adj.* | synonym | diligent |

You need to be smart and hardworking to get a job in that company.

❺ **aim** *n., v.*

The aim of the program is to improve your English listening skills.

We aim to raise sales by five percent.

❻ **loan** *n.*

We had to take out a loan to pay for the house.

❼ **finance** *n.*

He is an expert in finance. He teaches people how to make good use of their money.

EXTENSION **Other Usage of *Finance*:**

The activity is financed by the government. (*v.* provide money)

❽ **drop** *v.*

Two of my classes were at the same time, so I dropped one.

EXTENSION **Other Usages of *Drop*:**

A button dropped off my shirt. (means *fall*)

He dropped his schoolbag on the floor. (means *let something fall*)

Temperatures drop greatly at night in the mountains. (means *go down*)

❾ **negative** *adj.* | antonym | positive |

His drinking problem had a negative effect on his life.

❿ **advice** *n.*

The website provides lots of advice on baby care.

EXTENSION **advise** *v.*

My father advised me to wait until next year to buy a car.

advisor *n.* (also spelled as **adviser**)

The president's advisor has a lot of power.

A. Word Definitions

Use the clues to fill in the blanks with the word choices given. Change the word form if necessary.

midterm	semester	aim	loan	finance	deadline

1. I need to finish this paper before the final **deadline**. (time limit)
2. He's an expert in **finance**. That's why he's rich. (economics)
3. Leslie is studying hard for her history **midterm** next week. (test)
4. Rick got a big **loan** from the bank for his new car. (money you borrow)
5. I'm taking five courses this **semester**. (term)
6. Matthew **aims/aimed** to finish business school in two years. (plan)

B. Meanings in Context

Choose the meaning of the sentence in the conversation.

1. The midterms are coming up.
   a. They are arriving in a few days.
   (b.) There are some big tests soon.

2. I'm under a lot of stress.
   (a.) I'm worried and nervous.
   b. I'm hungry and thirsty.

3. The deadline is around the corner.
   a. It's on the other side of the street.
   (b.) There isn't much time left to do it.

4. Don't be so negative.
   a. You should exercise more.
   (b.) You should look on the bright side.

C. Words with Different Meanings

Match the word in bold with its definition.

1 I'm having **trouble** sending e-mails from my computer. ⓐ
Jane often **troubled** her parents to look after her baby son. ⓑ
Definition: ⓐ *n.* difficulty ⓑ *v.* to bother

2 Water from the roof **dropped** onto my head. ⓐ
I don't like history very much, so I **dropped** the course. ⓑ
Definition: ⓐ *v.* to fall ⓑ *v.* to stop studying

3 Once again, my brother **failed** to arrive on time. ⓑ
Jesse **failed** two of his exams this year. ⓐ
Definition: ⓐ *v.* to not pass ⓑ *v.* to not do something

D. Language Tips

Discussing Problems

I'm having	trouble with + Noun / Verb + -ing. difficulty + Verb + -ing. problems + Verb + -ing. a hard time + Verb + -ing.

Noun / Verb + -ing	is / are not easy. is / are difficult. is / are giving me a headache.

Use the information to practice the sentence patterns.

(prepare for) the final exams	(finish) my history paper	(study) German
(learn) this material	(set up) the new computer software	

Conditionals

Zero Conditional

We use the **zero conditional** when we talk about thing that are always true.

If + present simple, present simple

If you heat chocolate, it melts.
= Chocolate melts if you heat it.

If you study hard, you get good grade.
= You get good grade if you study hard.

If you eat too much, you gain weight.
= You gain weight if you eat too much.

Usage Note

When or **every time** has the same meaning as **if** in some zero conditional sentences.

If / **When** / **Every time** Sally drinks milk, she gets sick.

First Conditional

We use the **first conditional** when we talk about future events for real possibilities.

If + present simple, will + verb

If I have money, I will buy a new computer.
= I will buy a new computer if I have money.

If we win a contest, we will get the prize money.
= We will get the prize money if we win a contest.

If your boss likes you, he will let you take two weeks off.
= You boss will let you take two weeks off if he likes you.

Different Forms

	Condition	Result	Usage
If	I keep my job,	I **might** / **may** make it happen.	possibility
	you use the kitchen,	you **must** / **have to** do the dishes.	obligation
	she takes a plane,	she **should** ask for a window seat.	advice
	you have a driver's license,	you **can** / **may** drive.	permission
	someone calls,	tell them to call back later.	order

A. Fill in the Blanks

Write the correct form of each verb to complete the sentences.

1. Plants **die** (die) if they **don't get** (not get) enough water.
2. If the weather **is** (be) nice, we **will go** (go) to the park tomorrow.
3. If Emily **is** (be) late for work again, her boss **will get** (get) angry.
4. If you **lie** (lie) to people all the time, they **don't believe** (not believe) you any more.
5. My teacher **will get** (get) upset if the students **make** (make) noise.
6. If it **rains** (rain) tomorrow, Jerry and his friends **will not attend** (not attend) the outdoor concert.
7. If my daughter **eats** (eat) spicy food, her stomach **hurts** (hurt).
8. Dogs **bark** (bark) loudly if they **see** (see) a cat.

B. Match

Match the condition with the result.

d 1. If Laurie goes to bed after eleven,
f 2. If I get sick again,
h 3. If Ben doesn't have to work tomorrow,
g 4. If Maggie and her boyfriend sit in the front,
a 5. If your dad comes home before six o'clock,
b 6. If the room's temperature is too low,
e 7. If the bus is late,
c 8. If Bill walks to school,

a. ask him to give Uncle Bob a call.
b. I can't sleep.
c. he'll get some exercise.
d. she is tired the next day.
e. we might have to take a taxi.
f. I may need to see a doctor.
g. they will hear the music better.
h. he should come to the beach with us.

C. Correct the Mistakes

Fix the errors in the passage.

Student life can be full of stress. If students ~~won't~~ don't have a good balance between study, exercise, and rest, they usually have problems. They ~~didn't~~ **don't** get good grades if they ~~relaxed~~ **relax** too much. They don't remember as much if they ~~not~~ **do not** take regular breaks though.

Exercise is really important too. A student **will** study better and feel better if they go outside and play sports. If you ~~focusing~~ **focus** only on study, you might get worse grades! If you ~~wanted~~ **want** to do well in school, you should keep both your body and brain healthy.

Relaxed, healthy students are better learners. Remember, if you're tired, ~~taking~~ **take** a break. You remember much more if you ~~will~~ balance your time!

Worksheet

Task I

Choose the answers.

1. If you finish your dinner, you can / might have cake for dessert.
2. If Tina decides to get a car, she won't buy / doesn't buy a used one.
3. If it rains, we will get / must get wet.
4. If you go to France, you will / should visit Marseille.
5. If Leo doesn't come, Karen will be / was angry.
6. If she wakes up, will give / give me a call.
7. If Patrick wears those pants, the other students will laugh / laughed at him.
8. If we go on vacation, we can't / won't have enough time to visit your parents.

Task II

*Change the following into the **conditional sentences**.*

1. press that button / camera turn on (will)

   → ____

2. Ron is late / miss the boat (might)

   → ____

3. you use my car / bring it back early *(imperative)*

   → ____

4. my brother has enough money / buy a new scooter (will)

   → ____

5. you want to be finished before six o'clock / ask Winnie for help (should)

   → ____

6. the water begins to boil / turn the heat off *(imperative)*

   → ____

This page may be photocopied and distributed to the class.

Reading

Before You Read

Have you ever done an internship? Where would you like to do an internship?

Working for No Money

Track 55

While You Read

1. Why do students work for free?

2. What do Vatican interns receive?

Would you work for free? Most people would answer: "Absolutely not!" After all, it sounds unreasonable, right? However, a lot of Western college students work for no money. Instead of pay, they get experience, knowledge, and a better résumé. These jobs are called internships.

Many American university students take internships in their future fields. For example, sports or fashion majors would apply for an internship at Nike. People who are interested in film or computer science try for an internship with Pixar. There are plenty of opportunities.

Some well-known companies provide benefits with internships. Google interns have a better chance of getting a job later. Over a million people apply each year. The company usually hires just 2,000. Microsoft offers a 12-week internship. After they finish, interns can have a barbecue at Bill Gates' house! Interns for Southwest Airlines get free flights for the summer. Vatican interns report for the Catholic News Service. In return, they get free Italian lessons and the chance to live in a four-star hotel in Rome. These internships are really competitive, but they're also a great opportunity for students.

These days, internships are very popular. Ask your university about its internship program. It could change your life.

Key Words

❶ **absolutely** *adv.* | synonyms | certainly, definitely |

We absolutely need to get there tonight.

❷ **internship** *n.*

The record company is offering two summer internships.

EXTENSION **intern** *n., v.*

If you need coffee, just ask the intern.

I am interning at a computer company.

❸ **field** *n.*

Although Ted has a degree in marketing, he still has problems finding a job in his field.

EXTENSION **Other Usages of *Field*:**

There are 20 cows in the field. (means *an area of land on a farm*)

An American football field is around 91 meters long. (means *a grassy area for playing sports*)

❹ **apply** *v.*

I applied for a credit card last week.

EXTENSION **Usage Note**

> We **apply for** a job, a loan, or a thing. We **apply to** a company, a university, or any other place.
> You need to apply for a new driver's license.
> I'm going to apply to all of the universities on the list.

❺ **plenty of** *phr.* | synonym | lots of |

I don't need anything from the store. I have plenty of food at home.

❻ **well-known** *adj.* | synonym | famous |

Ernest Hemingway was a well-known American author. He wrote *The Old Man and the Sea*.

❼ **benefit** *n.*

The company gives its workers good medical benefits.

EXTENSION **Other Usage of *Benefit*:**

Many patients benefit from the new medicine. (*v.* get help)

❽ **in return** *phr.*

I give him guitar lessons, and he teaches me Spanish in return.

EXTENSION **Other Usage of *Return*:**

You didn't return my DVD. (*v.* give back)

A. Word Definitions

Use the clues to fill in the blanks with the word choices given. Change the word form if necessary.

absolutely	instead of	résumé	field	apply	plenty of	well-known	competitive

1. Let's eat pizza **instead of** noodles today. (as an alternative)
2. The medical **field** is rapidly growing. (area of study)
3. My internship experience will be the most important part of my **résumé**. (a list of achievements)
4. Dan's father is a(n) **well-known** Canadian actor. (famous)
5. You should **apply** for a visa two months before you travel. (request)
6. I **absolutely** love my job. The pay is good, and my boss is great. (certainly)
7. Professional football is a very **competitive** sport. (have a strong desire to win)
8. There are **plenty of** people in the park. (many)

B. Complete the Passage

Use the correct form of the words given to complete the passage.

experience	major	intern	benefit	internship

College is the best time in most people's lives. From drama to computer science 1. **majors**, college students can study all kinds of things. They study hard during the semester. Then students have vacation between each semester. Some students spend their summers traveling or relaxing, but today many of them want to do a(n) 2. **internship** in big companies. The job market isn't great, and a little real-world 3. **experience** can be an advantage. 4. **Interns** can see how a company works. They gain a good understanding of what the job is. Another 5. **benefit** is that they have a better chance of finding work when they finish college. Many companies prefer new employees with previous work experience.

C. True or False

*Check **True** or **False**.*

	True	False
1. Interns usually get paid a lot for their work.	☐	☑
2. Nike is a good choice for a fashion internship.	☑	☐
3. Film majors can go for an internship at Pixar.	☑	☐
4. There are not many types of internships available.	☐	☑
5. Google hires more than 3,000 workers per year.	☐	☑
6. Vatican interns get free flights once they finish their internships.	☐	☑
7. Universities usually have information on internships.	☑	☐
8. Students can get a lot of benefits from doing internships.	☑	☐

NOTES

Writing

TEACHER'S GUIDE 2

Writing

Task I *Below is a profile of Jenny and a short paragraph about her. Fill in the blanks.*

Name: Jenny Collins
Sex: female
Age: 18
School: New York University
Major: nursing
Year at school: freshman
Languages: English, French

Clubs: guitar, drama
Hobbies: playing the guitar, acting, singing, playing tennis
Favorite movie: *Alice in Wonderland*
Favorite TV show: *Glee*
Favorite singer / band: Radiohead
Favorite song: *Karma Police*
Future plans: work at a hospital

My name is **Jenny Collins**. I'm **18 years old** (age). I'm a student in my **first** year at **New York University**. I study **nursing**. I love my school! I have a lot of hobbies. I'm a member of the **guitar club and the drama club**. I like to **play the guitar**, **act**, **sing**, and **play tennis** in my free time. I enjoy watching movies. I like ***Alice in Wonderland*** the most. I also watch TV shows sometimes. My favorite program is ***Glee***. Music is very important to me. I usually listen to rock music. **Radiohead** is the best band in the world! I really love their song ***Karma Police***. After I graduate, I want to **work at a hospital**.

Task II *Fill in this profile. Write a short paragraph about yourself. Use Jenny's paragraph as an example.*

Put Photo Here

Name: ____________________
Sex: __________ Age: _____
School: ______________________________
Major: ______________ Year at school: ______________
Language(s): ______________________________

____
____
____
____
____

Writing

Task I *Read this introduction to Thanksgiving.*

Thanksgiving is an important holiday in the United States and Canada. People celebrate the Pilgrims' successful journey from Europe to the New World in 1621. Thanksgiving takes place in November. People meet with their entire family, cook a lot of food, and eat together. Many people live far away from each other, but they still try to get together on Thanksgiving Day. Traditional Thanksgiving foods include turkey, potatoes, sweet potatoes, sweet corn, and pumpkin pie. It's a day to eat a lot and relax with your family.

Use the introduction above as a sample. Write a short passage about Dragon Boat Festival. Make sure to answer the following questions.

1. What is Dragon Boat Festival?
2. When do people celebrate this festival?
3. What do people usually do (for example, race dragon boats, prepare rice dumplings, etc.)?
4. What are some of the traditional foods? What are they made of?

Task II *Look at the recipe below. Fill in the blanks using the words in the box.*

Thanksgiving Recipe: Sweet Potatoes

sweet potatoes	mix	make	bake	heat	place	add

To 1. **make** this dish, you need a bowl of 2. **sweet potatoes**, a quarter of a cup of orange juice, three quarters of a cup of flour, half a cup of sugar, some butter, and half a spoon of salt. 3. **Heat** the oven to 175 degrees. Put the sweet potatoes in a dish. 4. **Place** them in the oven. 5. **Add** some orange juice. 6. **Mix** sugar, butter, flour, and salt together in a bowl. Pour everything from the bowl on the sweet potatoes. 7. **Bake** for 30 to 40 minutes.

Create a recipe of your own and share it with the class.

Writing

Internet Language

Many people use Internet language when they talk online.

2: to
2day: today
2morrow: tomorrow
2nite: tonight
aite: alright
asap: as soon as possible
c: see
cmon: come on
cya: see you
h8: hate
h/w: homework
iasb: I am so bored
idk: I don't know
k: OK
kewl: cool
l8r: later
lol: laugh out loud
nm: not much
ntrly: not really
sup: what's up
syatp: see you at the party
pleez: please
thx: thanks
tmw: too much work
ur: you're
urtb: you are the best
wanna: want to

Change the conversation below into regular language.

Adam: Hey, Eva. Sup?
Eva: Nm. U?
Adam: I'm tired. I have h/w 2 do for 2morrow. ☹
Eva: Is it a lot?
Adam: Ntrly, but I just h8 math.
Eva: Ur so lazy! Lol. ☺ Wanna go c a movie 2nite?
Adam: Idk. I have tmw right now.
Eva: Pleez? Iasb 2day.
Adam: Aite. Let me finish my h/w first. Can I call u l8r?
Eva: Kewl. Let me know asap.

Adam: Hey, Eva. What's up?
Eva: Not much. You?
Adam: I'm tired. I have homework to do for tomorrow.
Eva: Is it a lot?
Adam: Not really, but I just hate math.
Eva: You're so lazy! (laughs out loud) Do you want to go see a movie tonight?
Adam: I don't know. I have too much work right now.
Eva: Please? I'm so bored today.
Adam: Alright. Let me finish my homework first. Can I call you later?
Eva: Cool. Let me know as soon as possible.

Change the following conversation into Internet language.

Kate: I am having a party tonight. You're invited. Bring your friends too!
Sam: Sounds cool. But I have classes tomorrow morning.
Kate: Come on. I need you there. You can come for a few hours.
Sam: OK, I will.
Kate: Thanks! You are the best. 😁
Sam: Alright. See you at the party.
Kate: OK. See you later then.

Kate: I am having a party 2nite. Ur invited. Bring your friends too!
Sam: Sounds kewl. But I have classes 2morrow morning.
Kate: Cmon. I need u there. U can come for a few hours.
Sam: K, I will.
Kate: Thx! Urtb.
Sam: Aite. Syatp.
Kate: K. Cya l8r then.

Writing

Task I *An ad company is looking for new models. Fill in the blanks using words from this unit.*

A

Model Needed

We are looking for a female model for a beer advertisement. She should be 1. **slender** (she can't be overweight). We need someone 2. **young** (between 18 and 24 years old). She should have 3. **long**, 4. **straight**, 5. **blonde** hair. She can't have short, curly, or black hair.

B

Man Wanted for Ad

A car company needs a male model for a sales video. We want someone 1. **tall**. His height should be at least 180 centimeters. He can have 2. **long** or 3. **short** hair. The length of his hair is not important. We also need someone 4. **fit**. He should have a big, strong body.

C

Lost Your Hair? Work for Us!

HAIR4U is looking for an actor for a hair product ad. He must be at least 50 years old. He also should be 1. **bald**. He can't have much hair. He can be 2. **tall** or 3. **short**. His height doesn't matter. It's OK for him to be a little 4. **overweight**, but he shouldn't be too fat.

Task II *Choose one product from below. Pretend you need a model for an ad. Write an ad like the ones above.*

Title: **(Sample Answer)**

We want to hire a female model for a cell phone advertisement. The model should be fit and tall. She should be at least 170 centimeters tall. We are looking for someone with a beautiful face and a slim body. She should also have long curly hair. Those with straight hair should not apply.

Writing

Task I *You are a nurse. Fill in the blanks in the note.*

health problem	symptoms	treatment
back injury	back pain hard to move hurts to stand	bed rest for a week cold pack twice a day massage slow exercises aspirin, two pills, three times a day with food

Note:

The patient has a back injury. He has a lot of 1. back pain. He also finds it difficult 2. to move. His back 3. hurts when he stands. He needs to 4. rest in bed for 5. seven days. He should also take two 6. pills of aspirin with 7. food, 8. three times each day. He might want to get a(n) 9. massage and do 10. slow exercise.

Task II *Answer the following questions and write a complete paragraph. Use some of the expressions below.*

once a year every (*number*) years / months / weeks	yesterday last month / year / winter two months ago in July / 2018	runny nose fever cough sore throat muscle pain	don't go to work / school rest in bed have a lot of water drink orange juice eat soup get more sleep avoid public places

a. How often do you get a cold?
b. When was the last time you had a cold?
c. What symptoms did you have?
d. What did the doctor tell you to do?
e. What did you do to feel better when you were sick?
f. What medicine did you take? How often did you take it? How much did you take?
g. How long did it take you to get healthy?

Read your paragraph to a partner. Help each other to fix any mistakes.

Writing

Task I *Below are reviews of two movies. Use the words from the box to fill in the blanks.*

funny	movie theater	runs	about	leading actors
should	boring	directed	comedy	action

A ***Little Fockers* Review**

This movie is the third in a series. The 1. **leading actors** in this movie are Ben Stiller and Robert De Niro. Paul Weitz is the director. This movie is 2. **about** a married couple with two children. The father of the children works with a beautiful woman. That woman is interested in him. This is a(n) 3. **comedy**. The actors are pretty good, but some of the jokes are not 4. **funny**. It's not a bad movie, but you shouldn't go to the 5. **movie theater** to watch it. You can watch it at home.

B ***Harry Potter and the Deathly Hallows* Review**

This is the seventh Harry Potter movie. It stars Daniel Radcliffe and Emma Watson. It is a story about a school of wizards. Harry Potter prepares to fight his enemy Lord Voldemort. The film was 1. **directed** by David Yates. He did a good job. It 2. **runs** for two and a half hours. That's a bit too long. That's why parts of the movie are a little 3. **boring**. Other parts are still a lot of fun. There are many fights and great 4. **action** scenes. If you like Harry Potter, you 5. **should** see this movie.

Task II *Choose a movie and write a review. Answer the questions in complete sentences.*

a. What is the movie about?
b. Who are the stars of the movie?
c. Who is the director of the movie?
d. What kind of movie is it (action, comedy, drama, etc.)?
e. What do you think about the movie? Is it boring, exciting, or intelligent?
f. Should people spend money and go to see it? Why or why not?

________________ *(Movie Name)* **Review**

____

____

____

____

____

____

____

Writing

Task I *Read these descriptions of special moments in Rick's life. Fill in the blanks using the words below.*

interesting	lonely	friend	nervous	thankful
cheer	worried	happiest	proud	saddest

A

The 1. **saddest** day of my life was when my dog Leo died. That was four years ago. He was very sick. I was really 2. **worried** about him.

One week later, he passed away. He was more than just a dog. He was my best 3. **friend**. I felt 4. **lonely** without him. I cried a lot. My friends helped to 5. **cheer** me up. They called me every day. I felt 6. **thankful** to them. It's good to have friends when you feel sad.

B

My first day at the university was the 1. **happiest** day of my life. My parents were very 2. **proud** of me. They always expected me to be successful. I met my roommates at the dorms. They were both 3. **interesting** people. It felt fantastic to make new friends. I was excited to start school. I was also 4. **nervous**. This was my first time away from home. I finally became an adult.

Task II *Complete Rick's story of his scary experience. Use the hints and your imagination.*

The scariest time of my life was when I got lost in a forest. It happened when I was 19. I went hiking alone. I didn't pay attention to the time. *(Now finish the story.)*

(Sample Answer)

a. **Suddenly, it got really dark.** (dark)

b. **I felt really scared.** (scared)

c. **It was very cold.** (cold)

d. **I was afraid of freezing to death.** (freezing to death)

e. **However, I found a warm cave.** (warm cave)

f. **I fell asleep in the cave.** (fell asleep)

g. **In the morning, I managed to find a road.** (morning, find, road)

h. **A car stopped.** (car)

i. **The driver gave me a ride home.** (gave, ride home)

j. **I felt so happy and relieved!** (happy, relieved)

Writing

Task I *Write about your free-time activity. Use the sentence patterns below.*

1. What is the activity?	In my free time, I enjoy + Verb + -ing. My favorite activity is + Verb + -ing.
2. Whom do you do it with?	I usually + Verb with my friends. My family and I often + Verb on the weekend.
3. Why do you like it?	I like + Noun / Verb + -ing + because . . . Noun / Verb + -ing is fun.
4. How often do you do it?	I + Verb + three times a week. I spend every weekend + Verb + -ing.
5. How much does it cost?	I spend (*money*) every time I + Verb. It costs (*money*) to Verb.

____

____

____

____

____

Task II *Janet is writing an e-mail to Mike. Fill in the blanks.*

discount	hip-hop	club	plan	free	pop	once	clubbing	charge

Hey Mike,

How are you? Are you 1. ___free___ this weekend? I know you like to party. I often go 2. ___clubbing___ with my friends on Saturdays because I like to dance. Would you like to come to a 3. ___club___ with us this weekend? There is a cool place near my house. They play 4. ___pop___ music and 5. ___hip-hop___. I go there at least 6. ___once___ a month. The cover 7. ___charge___ is $20, but I know the owner. We would get a 8. ___discount___. We spend around $10 every time we go. Dancing is always fun. Does this sound like a 9. ___plan___? Let me know ASAP.

Best regards,

Janet

Writing

Task I *Look at Cristiano Ronaldo's profile. Fill in the blanks with the information given.*

Cristiano Ronaldo

Photo: nimAdestiny / Flickr

Sport	Soccer
Nationality	Portuguese
Position	Forward, midfielder
Former club Years	Manchester United 2003 — 2009
Current club Years	Real Madrid 2009 — present
Awards	FIFA's Player of the Year, 2008 Three Premier League championships One Champions League cup
Annual salary	About $18,000,000

Biography

Cristiano Ronaldo is a famous 1. **Portuguese** soccer player. He plays for 2. **Real Madrid**. He also played for Manchester United from 3. **2003** to 4. **2009**. He 5. **won** three Premier League championships and a Champions League cup. He received FIFA's Player of the Year Award in 2008. Ronaldo makes about $18 6. **million** a year.

Task II *Work with a partner to complete the following conversation. Use the words given.*

Sport
soccer
basketball
baseball

Position
goalkeeper, forward, midfielder, defender
guard, forward, center
pitcher, catcher, first base, second base, third base

A: What is your favorite sport?
B: **I like playing soccer**. What's yours?
A: I really like **baseball**.
B: That's cool. Do you play or watch?
A: I **prefer to watch**.
B: Which **team is your favorite** (team, favorite)?
A: **My favorite team is the New York Mets**. What about you?
B: **My favorite is Chelsea**.
Who **is your favorite player** (favorite, player)?
A: I'm a huge fan of **Francisco Rodríguez**.
He **is a pitcher** (position). And you?
B: My favorite **player is Petr Čech**.
He **is a goalkeeper** (position).

Writing

Task I

Use the correct form of the words to fill in the blanks in the report about a snowstorm.

snow	temperature	die	avoid	damage
prepare	experience	wind	last	cover

Our town 1. experienced a snowstorm last week. The 2. temperature was minus 15 degrees Celsius. We had heavy 3. snow and strong 4. wind. It was blowing at a speed of 120 kilometers per hour, so we couldn't see anything. The roads were 5. covered by snow. Driving was impossible. There was some 6. damage to the power lines, and many people didn't have electricity. Lots of trees fell down. Luckily, we were warned about the storm and were 7. prepared. We bought food and water ahead of time. Everybody 8. avoided going outside. The storm 9. lasted for two days. Many houses were damaged by the wind and the snow. The good news is that nobody 10. died!

Task II

Imagine that your city will be hit by a typhoon. Write a weather warning in ***the future tense.***

This is a weather warning. A typhoon will reach our area tomorrow. (reach, tomorrow)

There will be heavy rain with thunder and lightning. (rain, thunder, lightning)

More than 200 millimeters of rain will fall. (200 millimeters of rain)

The wind will be very strong at a speed of 140 kilometers per hour. (wind, strong, speed, 140 kilometers)

This will be dangerous. (dangerous)

You need to buy extra food and water. (need, food, water)

You will probably have no electricity. (probably, no electricity)

You should buy a flashlight. (buy, flashlight)

Check the radio for weather reports. (radio, weather reports)

We'll have updates every 30 minutes (updates, 30 minutes)

Stay safe out there.

Writing

Task I *Below is a restaurant review. Use the correct form of the words to fill in the blanks.*

date	dessert	starter	service	parking	favorite
baked	recommend	open	salty	accept	wine

La Parisienne is a new French restaurant. I went there last week. The waiter 1. **recommended** the onion soup and the duck breast with 2. **baked** potatoes. I accepted his suggestion. I also ordered a tomato salad as a(n) 3. **starter**. It was great. The onion soup was tasty but a little 4. **salty**. The duck was perfectly cooked. That was my 5. **favorite** dish of the night. For 6. **dessert**, I had a piece of chocolate cake. I loved it. I washed my meal down with a nice glass of 7. **wine**. It was an excellent dining experience. This is not a cheap restaurant, but it's a good place for a(n) 8. **date**.

General Info:

The 9. **service** is friendly and quick. The restaurant 10. **accepts** all credit cards. It takes reservations over the phone or online. There is 11. **parking** in the back. It's 12. **open** from Monday to Saturday, from noon to 10:00 p.m.

Task II *Write a review of your favorite restaurant. Answer the following questions in your review.*

1. What type of food does it serve?
2. What is the most popular dish there?
3. What is your favorite (least favorite) dish, and why do (don't) you like it?
4. What is the best starter? How about dessert?
5. What general info can you provide?

Writing

Task I *Below is an ad for an internship. Use the correct form of the words to fill in the blanks.*

hardworking	intern	succeed	experience
résumé	interest	attitude	call

INTERNS NEEDED

BrandMark Inc. is a popular marketing company. With more than 30 years of 1. __experience__, we provide 2. __interns__ with lots of training. If you work for us, you will develop important real-world skills.

The perfect intern must have a(n) 3. __interest__ in business development. He or she shouldn't be lazy — we want someone 4. __hardworking__. Applicants need to have a positive 5. __attitude__ and try hard to 6. __succeed__. They must major in Business. If this is you, send a(n) 7. __résumé__ and a cover letter to David Gunning at dgunning@brandmark.com. No phone 8. __calls__, please.

Task II *Fill in the cover letter using the information in the ad above.*

Ken Carter
Résumé

Goal:
To find an internship in marketing

Education:
Brown University
B.A. in Business expected June 2017

Work Experience:
March 2014 to September 2014
Store Manager, Iscream, Providence

- Managed three salespeople
- Created business reports
- Helped to increase sales

School Record:
Third out of 120 in the Department of Business

Dear __Mr. Gunning__,

I am __a business student at Brown University__ (student). I will __graduate in June 2017__ (2017). I saw your ad online. I am interested in becoming an intern at your company. __I am one of the top three students in my class__ (top three). I study hard to get good grades, and I have a strong interest in business. I also __have a positive attitude__ (attitude). If I see a problem, I do everything to solve it. In addition, I have business experience. From March to September 2014, I worked as __store manager at the Iscream store in Providence__ (Iscream). During my time there, I __managed three salespeople__, __created business reports for the owner__, and __helped the store to increase sales__. I would be a great intern at BrandMark Inc. I hope to hear from you soon.

Best regards,
__Ken Carter__

WORKSHEETS – ANSWER KEY

UNIT 5

p. 73 Task I

1. smells 2. was 3. turns 4. sounded
5. looks / looked 6. tasted 7. becomes 8. remain

Task II

1. I made him **go** to bed for an hour.
2. The weather turned **cold** last week.
3. He seemed **happier** after eating.
4. My brother lets me **wear** his clothes sometimes.
5. There seems to be a problem with my car. I can't get it **to start**.
6. Alex's boss had him **work** on weekends.
7. We should get Chris **to buy** us some food when he goes to the store.
8. The teacher made her students **write** a story about their best friends.

UNIT 7

p. 101 Task I

1. Walking for so long is very tired / **tiring**.
2. The boy was **frightened** / frightening when he saw the spider.
3. Those pictures of me are really embarrassed / **embarrassing**.
4. The question is too confused / **confusing**. I don't understand it.
5. Henry was **shocked** / shocking after he heard the news.
6. My dog gets **excited** / exciting if I pick up his food bowl.

Task II

1. in
2. about
3. by
4. of
5. with
6. with

UNIT 12

p. 171

Task I

1. If you finish your dinner, you **can** / might have cake for dessert.
2. If Tina decides to get a car, she **won't buy** / doesn't buy a used one.
3. If it rains, we **will get** / must get wet.
4. If you go to France, you will / **should** visit Marseille.
5. If Leo doesn't come, Karen **will be** / was angry.
6. If she wakes up, will give / **give** me a call.
7. If Patrick wears those pants, the other students **will laugh** / laughed at him.
8. If we go on vacation, we can't / **won't** have enough time to visit your parents.

Task II

1. If you press that button, the camera will turn on.
2. If Ron is late, he might miss the boat.
3. If you use my car, bring it back early.
4. If my brother has enough money, he will buy a new scooter.
5. If you want to be finished before six o'clock, you should ask Winnie for help.
6. If the water begins to boil, turn the heat off.